Praise for Lead to Disrupt

This is what leading business, academic, political, industry and community leaders, along with entrepreneurs and board directors are saying:

Lead to Disrupt is a call to action for all leaders. Kumar Parakala's emphasis on agility, adaptability, and a proactive approach to challenging the status quo and mindset strikes a chord with me. His plea for a shift from conventional leadership structures towards collaborative, inclusive frameworks that spark creativity and innovation is pertinent and indispensable in today's ever-changing world.

The Hon. Nelson W. Wolff | American judge | Texas state senator and legislator (fmr)

Kumar Parakala adeptly delves into the intricacies of organizational dynamics and cultural metamorphosis, presenting practical strategies for leaders seeking to maneuver through the obstacles of the ever-changing business environment. Parakala's engaging writing style simplifies intricate leadership principles, making them accessible and applicable to for-profit and nonprofit organizations alike. An essential guide for modern leaders, Parakala's book teaches how to turn volatility into a competitive advantage.

Daniel Keller | Deputy chairman of executive board and COO, Berliner Volksbank

Kumar Parakala's *Lead to Disrupt* provides a transformative outlook on leadership, urging a departure from conventional approaches and advocating for the adoption of innovative principles and actions to foster progress and expansion in organizations and society. With astute observations and actionable advice, Parakala effectively champions a reimagining of leadership for today's dynamic landscape.

Ron Nirenberg | Mayor of San Antonio, Texas, USA

Many of us have come to appreciate the difficult times we live in, but how to navigate them in our roles is not easy. Geopolitics, environmental issues, social inequalities, and unrest are some of the issues we face. Strong and effective leadership has always been critical to helping us through challenges thrown at us. Right now, it seems we are facing them all at once. Leadership needs to be dynamic and transformative. Kumar has written an exceptional road map for these dynamic and difficult times for us to see things differently and act with passion and conviction as leaders. I encourage everyone to read this book to help them be a better leader in these disruptive times. We owe it to ourselves to be better in our leadership.

Egidio Zarrella | Senior partner, KPMG

Traditional leadership models are increasingly ineffective in our post-Covid, AI-driven, Gen-Z world. Kumar presents a bold and disruptive leadership approach tailored to modern challenges. His seven-key formula is invaluable for leaders across all sectors—public and private organizations, nonprofits, educational institutions, and government. This book is beneficial for C-level executives, corporate leaders, team leaders, entrepreneurs, and aspiring leaders alike. Kumar's insights are drawn from decades of hands-on management and leadership experience, enriched by lessons from the school of hard knocks. A must-read for leaders of every stripe!

Dr. Prasad Kodukula | CEO, NeoChloris | PMI Fellow | *USA Today* **best-selling author of eleven books**

Lead to Disrupt offers insights on a new way of being on leadership strategies to navigate constant global digital disruption and change. On his life journey, Parakala explored the depths of mental conditioning and mindset that shape our perception and our reality. His wisdom and philosophy on resilience, agility, innovation, alignment with a disruptive higher purpose and positive mindset is a game-changer in the face of obstacles and adversity.

Anthony Wong | President, IFIP

Kumar Parakala's insights into disruptive leadership are a game-changer. This book equips leaders with the mindset and tools needed to challenge the status quo and achieve extraordinary results.

Aaron Vick | Multi-X founder | Startup advisor | author

A groundbreaking book that reimagines leadership for the digital age. Parakala's actionable advice on fostering a disruptive mindset is indispensable.

Shawn Johal | Business growth coach | Best-selling author

Kumar Parakala's insights into developing a disruptive mindset are both profound and practical. This book is a must-read for those who aspire to lead organizations in the digital age.

Prof. Dr Rob Fijneman | CEO, KPMG Netherlands (fmr) | Partner at KPMG Switzerland | Professor, Tias School for Business and Society

From embracing innovation to fostering collaboration, *Lead to Disrupt* is packed with insights that are crucial for leading in the twenty-first century.

Tamara Nall | CEO and founder, The Leading Niche

Kumar Parakala's approach to leadership is revolutionary based on his own life experiences. His emphasis on continuous transformation and bold vision is exactly what today's leaders need.

Sheba Nandkeolyar | CEO, MultiConnexions Group | President, IAA | Board Director

Lead to Disrupt by Kumar Parakala is a transformative guide that breaks barriers, shifts mindsets, and champions collaboration and inclusivity. Drawing from his lived experiences, Kumar shows how building disruptive relationships and networks unlocks new opportunities and resources to serve others. This book is essential for those seeking significant personal and professional growth.

Suhail Arastu | Arts commissioner | Marshall fellow | Community leader

Employees today respond to leaders in different ways, suggesting that no single leadership style is universally successful. Kumar Parakala highlights the importance of thinking innovatively and possessing various nontraditional capabilities to lead a business in his book *Lead to Disrupt*. Drawing from his extensive experience as a leader across both emerging and mature industries, Parakala shares insights that have proven effective in the turbulent business environment of modern economies. This book offers novel strategies for both new and experienced leaders and CEOs planning to take their organizations to the next level of success.

Proffessor Lee Di Milia | Dean, School of Business and Law, Central Queensland University

A transformative guide that challenges traditional leadership paradigms, Kumar Parakala's book is a crucial resource for thriving in our unpredictable world.

Phil Bradley | Board director | Global CFO (ret.), GHD

Kumar's deep understanding of leadership in a disruptive era is both enlightening and inspiring. *Lead to Disrupt* is an essential read for anyone looking to make a significant impact. I agree a hundred percent with Kumar's insights and guidance! Any executive with business transformation leadership responsibilities will benefit significantly from this book.

Stephen G Hasty Jr | Partner and global transformation leader (ret.), KPMG

This book is a beacon for leaders at every level, offering invaluable guidance on how to harness disruption to drive meaningful change.

Mirjana D Perko | CEO, Incon

For leaders aspiring to instigate significant change and facilitate growth within their organizations, *Lead to Disrupt* is an essential reading. Kumar Parakala's astute observations and actionable tactics based on real-life experiences provide a blueprint for maneuvering through the intricacies of contemporary leadership and igniting transformative results.

Sheree Waterson | Chief product officer (fmr), Athleta | Ex-CPO, Lululemon

Lead to Disrupt by Kumar R. Parakala is a call to action, challenging us to embrace the uncertainty that defines our new normal. This book offers a fresh perspective on how leaders need to not only anticipate and adapt to disruption but also harness it to drive meaningful change.
Joseph Holtgreive | A/Dean, McCormick School of Engineering | Co-director, Personal Development StudioLab, Northwestern University

Kumar Parakala's *Lead to Disrupt* is a blueprint for modern leadership. His emphasis on diversity and inclusion as drivers of innovation is both timely and necessary.
Trissa Tismal-Capili | *USA Today and Wall Street Journal-***bestselling author | Founder, Institute of Conscious Business Leaders**

LEAD to DISRUPT

7 KEYS TO SUCCESS IN A CHANGING WORLD

KUMAR R. PARAKALA

Copyright © 2024 Kumar R. Parakala
Published in the United States by Leaders Press.
www.leaderspress.com

All rights reserved. No part of this book may be reproduced or transmitted in any form or by any means, electronic or mechanical, including photocopying, recording, or by an information storage and retrieval system—except by a reviewer who may quote brief passages in a review to be printed in a magazine or newspaper—without permission in writing from the publisher.

ISBN **978-1-63735-263-2** (hcv)
ISBN **978-1-63735-261-8** (pbk)
ISBN **978-1-63735-262-5** (ebook)

Library of Congress Control Number: **2023916462**

To Paddy, Sreya, JP, and Manish:
May our bond flourish evermore with each passing day.
With heartfelt love and boundless gratitude!

Proceeds from the sale of this book will be donated to support future leaders, youth groups, and performing artists through GHD Foundation and Musical Bridges Around the World.

Table of Contents

Preface 13

Chapter 1: What Disruptive Leaders Do and Why 17

Chapter 2: Developing the Disruptive Mindset 39

Chapter 3: Find a Disruptive Higher Purpose 67

Chapter 4: Disrupt Your Comfort Zone and Inertia 91

Chapter 5: Build Relationships That Foster
  Disruptive Thinking 109

Chapter 6: Disrupt the Status Quo 129

Chapter 7: Mental Resilience: Conquering
  Complacency and Fragility 147

Chapter 8: What Accountability Means and Why
  Results Matter 167

Chapter 9: Turning the Seven Keys 185

About the Author 201

Preface

Today, the world is changing at an astonishing pace, as unforeseen events and crises unfold almost every day, leaving us bewildered. As I wrote this book, we're still reeling from a pandemic that spread across the globe in a matter of months, disrupting our lives in unprecedented ways. Its impact still reverberates through every organization and has touched the lives of every individual. As the pandemic seemed to be finally coming under control, a stock market crash shook the financial landscape, causing millions to lose significant portions of their net worth.

Amidst this upheaval, the effects of climate change revealed themselves through the emergence of the La Niña event, evidenced by the eight warmest years ever recorded, the melting of glaciers, and the rise of sea levels. Natural disasters such as bushfires and flooding also became more frequent.

Racial tensions came to the forefront of global consciousness, highlighted by tragic events, such as the killing of George Floyd. His death sparked widespread outrage and ignited a demand for justice and an end to systemic racism. The incident served as a painful reminder of the glaring inequities experienced by marginalized communities and the urgent need for comprehensive reform. It prompted a collective call for meaningful dialogue, empathy, and concrete actions toward creating a more inclusive and equitable society where every individual can live without fear of discrimination or oppression.

As we grappled with all this, geopolitical tensions swelled with the Ukraine-Russia war and the deterioration of relationships between China and other leading nations. Just as efforts were being made to resolve the Ukraine crisis and restore relations with China, an unexpected attack by Hamas on Israel escalated the Middle East conflict, putting an abrupt halt to years of peace negotiations.

During these tumultuous events, November 2022 witnessed the launch of ChatGPT, the first generative artificial intelligence (GenAI) platform, which attracted 100 million users in just two months. Numerous studies predict that it would eliminate 14 percent of jobs and transform another 30 percent in the next three years with further advancements in GenAI technologies and machine intelligence. In October 2023, interest rates reached unprecedented levels, forcing many to put their home on sale in the coming months.

In January 2020, as all this turmoil began, we moved to the United States to expand our startup business, which was growing rapidly. Fueled by ambition, resilience, and a desire to be closer to our daughter, a student at Northwestern University in Illinois, we uprooted ourselves from Australia, our home for thirty years, and embarked on a new chapter of our entrepreneurial journey.

Little did we know that fate had a different plan in store for us. Within three months of relocating, lockdowns and border restrictions came into force, throwing a wrench in our carefully laid plans. The very essence of business—in-person meetings, collaborations, and engagement—became impossible, and we spent long hours in front of computers. Like many leaders, the challenge of growing our global business in a world full of obstacles presented itself, demanding a mindset shift and leadership approach that we never anticipated.

This time of isolation and prolonged uncertainty took a toll on our mental health and well-being. The weight of responsibility rested heavily on my shoulders as I navigated the dual task of ensuring the welfare of my team while striving to expand our business amid endless adversity.

During these trying times, I began to question how to lead. How could I effectively steer my team and safeguard the well-being of our organization in a world where unforeseen forces collide with personal circumstances? How could I rise above the chaos and become a beacon of strength, hope, and stability?

In my search for answers, I realized that true leadership goes beyond merely surviving challenges. It involves thriving while surrounded by adversity. Resilience, adaptability, and a growth mindset emerged as essential traits for navigating our frequently disruptive and volatile world. I learned the significance of fostering open communication, empathy, and connection within my team while cultivating a supportive environment that nurtured both business growth and individual well-being. I concluded that in a world where crises seem to arise daily, leaders must continually adapt to the unexpected.

Effective leadership now had to encompass more than delivering financial results. Effective leadership also has to prioritize the well-being of oneself and others.

Amidst the complexity and uncertainty of today's business landscape, traditional leadership models have become inadequate, hindering the progress of corporate leaders—myself included. The emergence of socially and environmentally conscious generations, combined with rapid technological advancements, demanded a fresh approach to leadership. This new approach must effectively navigate intricate business dynamics, drive profitability, and encourage change across outdated models, products, services, and, most importantly, culture.

In short, it must disrupt the way things are done in favor of a more effective way.

Leaders who aspire to "future-proof" their organizations face a myriad of obstacles, such as entrenched silos, outdated technology, skill gaps, cultural barriers, and financial limitations. Today, it's essential for leaders to embody a broader, more far-reaching vision, anticipate coming trends, swiftly embrace evolving technologies, carefully manage diverse workforces spanning cultures and generations; and, above all, deliver marketable results for the benefit of all stakeholders, not just shareholders.

It's a tall order for which many leaders are neither prepared nor trained. Therefore, this book embarks on an exploration of the evolving demands placed on leaders, advocating for a new paradigm of thinking. I implore leaders to honor their current roles while actively embracing and implementing necessary changes to tackle the challenges of disruption proactively. This transformative journey is akin to replacing engines midflight. It demands meticulous management of organizational evolution—one step at a time—all while ensuring uninterrupted delivery of existing plans.

As I've seen all this unfold, I've found myself questioning how leaders can effectively guide and safeguard their organizations, as well as themselves, after years of being entrenched in traditional corporate cultures. These forces not only challenge our conventional understanding of leadership, but they also compel us to reassess the very essence of what it means to lead. In the face of such pervasive disruptions, can we truly adhere to unchanged leadership approaches? Organizations must now swiftly evolve, adapt, innovate, and undergo permanent transformation to shift from mere survival today to flourishing tomorrow.

What type of leaders do we need amidst this relentless acceleration of these forces? This book offers insights and strategies for navigating the ever-changing landscape and recommends ways to create meaningful change by embracing a new mode of leadership.

The answer, in principle, is easy:

Disruptive times require disruptive leaders!

CHAPTER 1
What Disruptive Leaders Do and Why

Here are my key objectives in writing this book:

- Provide insights on how to challenge traditional leadership models and embrace new leadership principles and behaviors to drive change and growth
- Offer practical strategies to navigate and lead in an increasingly dynamic and uncertain business environment based on "lived experiences"
- Inspire leaders to think outside the box, break through barriers, and create new opportunities for themselves and their organizations by providing examples of what has worked in the ever-changing world
- Help leaders understand the importance of fostering a culture of innovation and empowerment within their teams
- Challenge leaders to continuously learn and evolve, fostering a growth mindset and embracing lifelong learning as essential traits for disruptive leadership

That said, here are the issues that propelled me to write this book.

Unprecedented Societal and Business Changes

In the twenty-first century, we have seen massive changes affecting almost every aspect of society. Facing those changes all at once opens the door to massive disruptions in the economy. On the surface, that sounds like very bad news, but the Cold War in the 1950s brought us the Space Race of the 1960s, and that brought us the micro-electronics revolution that disrupted every aspect of our lives—for the better!

The capability to see and adapt business practices to new technologies and societal expectations is rapidly becoming the key differentiator between economic success and failure.

Since 2020, when COVID-19 first thrust itself into our lives, a huge change has taken place, perhaps as big for our culture as the micro-electronics revolution was for our technology. Its effects have been unprecedented in our lifetimes. The lockdowns, safety measures, and obligations imposed on our society have forced us to think, work, and live very different lives than any of us expected. Most of us have lived in stable conditions all our lives. The COVID protocols were unlike anything the human race experienced since the Spanish flu pandemic following World War I.

We are still dealing with some remnants of COVID protocols and the mindset of fear and uncertainty in many people. Some still wear masks and gloves in public. Some have lost all trust in the government, and many businesses closed permanently. As the economy opened up, many chose to retire instead of returning to work, which altered America's workforce dramatically and will continue to do so for years.

All this was incredibly rapid, unlike most recent changes. For example, horses and buggies evolved into internal combustion autos, and now the potential of electric cars.

COVID-19 startled us, forcing us to rethink the journey of humanity. Despite our medical advancements, most of us sat in mandatory shutdown for eighteen to twenty-four months. It proved that despite what we thought we were good at, we had difficulty dealing with a potential global disaster. The pandemic highlighted serious inadequacies in conventional wisdom and business best practices. It showed us our conventions and practices were not necessarily wise or the best. For me, it was time for self-reflection and an opportunity to make tough changes under difficult circumstances. I feel it was a time that added to my maturity. It was also a period of learning that much is possible when necessity drives invention. The successful shift of hundreds of millions of in-office workers to remote workers defied belief. We learned that it was the human mindset, especially among leaders, that held us back, not the technology or management capability. Advanced technology has made remote work possible, but imagine, if you can, doing what we did with a dial-up internet service and no teleconferencing! The tech was there; we simply hadn't thought to make full use of its capabilities.

The COVID period has since seen an incredible acceleration of the digital movement, with people realizing much more was possible in the *virtual world*, or *cyberspace* as we call it. Surprisingly, this digital acceleration also made human contact precious as we had to work harder to know people and build relationships. Employees now actively evaluate if companies live by the values they advocate, and if not, they do not hesitate to quit, resulting in the Great Resignation phenomenon. It's an indictment of corporate culture. People have become bolder in dealing with the unknown and are challenging the power dynamics. Leaders like myself started embracing vulnerability.

At the same time, the world's infrastructure—powerplants, utility grids, roads, dams—continued to age, and leaders at all political levels began to truly realize that we have not been making an adequate investment in its maintenance. Much of the western world's infrastructure is between fifty and one hundred years old. Aged structures require more repairs, and some require expansion to meet increasing community needs; some just need replacing. All of that requires spending money that politicians prefer to spend elsewhere. Because the government has increasingly spent money on social welfare and other areas, it has not prioritized infrastructure spending for a long time. Looking at the global economy, infrastructure challenges are common in developing countries. They need more and better infrastructure, but they do not have the money to build it. It's a vicious cycle challenge—without that infrastructure, their economies cannot grow to generate the money needed for new infrastructure.

Climate change and alternative energy have become hot-button issues in every political campaign and most business planning. Energy transition from coal, natural gas, and oil to hydrogen, solar, and wind is a priority for many. Solar and hydrogen power have been around for decades, and water and wind have been around for millennia, but carbon-based fuels still account for 60.2 percent of power generation in the US. Renewables (solar, wind, etc.) are collectively second at 21.5 percent, with nuclear providing 18.2 percent.[1]

If carbon-based fuels are going to end as the power-generation source of choice, a whole new infrastructure must be built—that means a huge investment of resources. While the need for energy transition investment has been acknowledged by most countries, the total investment required is forecast to be around US$4 trillion per year for decades to come. The financial and workforce resources needed are incredible.

Likewise, the international supply chain became almost hopelessly mired during the lockdowns and has still not fully recovered. Supply chain resilience now commands the attention of every manufacturer with widespread suppliers, distributors, and retailers. As I write this book (in late 2023), an industry survey concluded, "More than half of logistics managers surveyed by CNBC do not expect the supply chain to return to normal until 2024 or after."[2]

The Cold War with the Soviet Union—not to mention the USSR itself—ended decades ago, but we now seem to find ourselves in another cold war with China,[3] even as Russia strains to conquer Ukraine and the war against terrorism continues, especially after the latest explosion of terrorism against Israel

---

[1] "What is U.S. electricity generation by energy source?" *EIA.gov*. Washington DC: US Energy Information Administration, February 2023. https://www.eia.gov/tools/faqs/faq.php?id=427&t=3, accessed 3 August 2023.
[2] Lori Ann LaRocco, "Most supply chain managers expect problems to continue at least through 2024," *CNBC.com*. New York City: Comcast and NBCUniversal News Group, 23 December 2022. https://www.cnbc.com/2022/12/23/supply-chain-managers-expect-problems-continue-2024.html, (accessed 3 August 2023).
[3] Andrea Rizzi, "A new Cold War between the US and China is spreading around the world," *ElPais.com*. Madrid, Spain: Promotora de Informaciones, SA, 19 February 2023. https://english.elpais.com/international/2023-02-19/a-new-cold-war-between-the-us-and-china-is-spreading-around-the-world.html, accessed 3 August 2023. [To name just one such opinion.]

by Hamas in Gaza. Geopolitical pressures have increased so much that some wonder if they ever actually decreased.

Most challenging of all are the economic pressures on individuals and families. "Consumer prices for all items rose 6.5 percent from December 2021 to December 2022," says the Consumer Price Index official report[4], but some commodity prices doubled, or more, since 2021. People who invested in the stock market lost trillions of dollars of net worth.[5] People are constantly talking about their economic outlook, recession, the decline of the stock market, and the accompanying stress.

The implications of these changes are far-reaching and threaten to seriously challenge the fabric of society. Many are calling this a VUCA society—one plagued by *volatility*, *uncertainty*, *complexity*, and *ambiguity*.

Market and social forces have always been part of life. But other than during the world wars, few in recent generations have needed to deal with simultaneous challenges in such numbers, in such rapidity, and with so many interconnections. Such times breed opportunities as well as challenges (both in the long and short term) for individuals, communities, and organizations to evolve. Such evolution, by its nature, demands a new kind of evolutionary leadership.

Disruptive Forces Shaping Our World

Disruptive forces are shaping the world and our businesses in unexpected and unpredictable ways. These are permanently changing the way we operate—not just in business, but also

---

[4] "Consumer Price Index: 2022 in review," *BLS.gov*. Washington DC: US Department of Labor, 17 January 2023. https://www.bls.gov/opub/ted/2023/consumer-price-index-2022-in-review.htm (accessed 3 August 2023).

[5] Irina Ivanova, "Stock market's fall has wiped out $3 trillion in retirement savings this year," *CBSNews.com*. New York City: CBS News, Inc., 17 June 2022. https://www.cbsnews.com/news/stocks-drop-recession-retirement-savings-401k-ira-3-trillion-2022 (accessed 3 August 2023).

across society and as individuals. The changes are irreversible and force people to identify new ways to survive and thrive.

COVID is the number-one recent disruptive force, changing the lives of almost everyone across the world. It revealed the fragility of humankind but also drove an explosive pace of innovation. Human beings demonstrated their determination to protect what they believed in.

Let us explore some of the unpredictable, disruptive forces that recently emerged and are profoundly reshaping our lives and businesses:

AI and Automation

The unstoppable rise of AI and automation is at the forefront. These technological advancements surpass our wildest dreams, challenging the boundaries of what we thought possible in the next five years. They threaten to replace human workers with intelligent machines, sparking a revolution that fundamentally changes the nature of work in every industry and fabric of our society. The impact is so significant that some industries risk obsolescence unless they swiftly adapt and transform.[6]

Geopolitical Tensions

Geopolitical tensions are significant disruptors, unsettling the global foundations of stability. The Ukraine-Russia conflict and Israel-Gaza attacks have unleashed economic instability, compelling companies to reevaluate their long-term strategies and prioritize immediate survival. The persistent friction between the United States and China poses a formidable threat to the global economy and hampers collective efforts

---

[6] Forrester's Report, "AI could replace 2.4 million jobs in US by 2030," *Dig. Watch*. Malta: DiploFoundation, 8 September 2023. https://dig.watch/updates/ai-will-replace-2-4-million-jobs-in-us-by-2030-forresters-report#:~:text=Generative%20AI%20is%20expected%20to,according%20to%20Forrester's%202023%20report, accessed 28 December 2023.

to address environmental challenges. The ongoing tensions between the two superpowers are driven by security concerns over national and digital domains, safeguarding citizens, and data privacy. This disrupts the supply chain and intensifies the quest for sovereignty and control. The pace of the global economy will likely slow as a result.

Remote Work

Since the lockdowns, remote work has become the norm for many individuals and companies. In this new paradigm, the boundaries separating work and personal lives decrease, offering both novel possibilities and obstacles. Organizations have become more agile and employee motivation to come to work has permanently changed. This shift has reshaped the idea of productivity and work-life equilibrium to empower individuals with greater control over when and how they approach labor. Employees are increasingly choosing how, where, when, and why they work.[7]

Climate Change and Sustainability

The urgent need to combat climate change is altering the fabric of our society. It's also reshaping investment priorities, resource acquisition, business plans, and job markets. Sustainability and renewable energy are now center stage, giving rise to green jobs that support our fight against the impending climate crisis. The World Health Organization warns that over 3.6 billion people already reside in climate change–vulnerable regions, which heightens the urgency to act.[8]

---

[7] [Unbylined], "Americans are embracing flexible work—and they want more of it," *McKinsey.com*. New York: McKinsey Insights, 23 June 2022. https://www.mckinsey.com/industries/real-estate/our-insights/americans-are-embracing-flexible-work-and-they-want-more-of-it, accessed 28 December 2023.

[8] Fact Sheets, "Climate change," *WHO.int*. Geneva, Switzerland: World Health Organization, 12 October 2023. https://www.who.int/news-room/fact-sheets/detail/climate-change-and-health, accessed 28 December 2023.

Platform and Gig Economy

The gig economy (freelancing) sweeps across industries, revolutionizing work and livelihoods. Platforms like Uber, Amazon, and Netflix have seamlessly integrated themselves into the lives of millions, offering greater independence and flexibility. Short-term contracts and freelance work are now common. A vibrant ecosystem of independent workers might also change our whole outlook on employment.

Demographic Shifts

Demographic shifts continually shape the world. Aging populations and declining birth rates mean workforce planning must adapt to these changes. In the United States alone, thousands of individuals reach the traditional retirement age every day, which underscores an urgent need to meet their changing needs. As Western countries witness a decline in skilled workers among younger generations, Asia—notably China and India—boasts a substantial generation of highly educated young people. Among China's 800-million-strong workforce, a quarter are highly skilled and young. For decades, Asian countries have prioritized education to foster workforce growth and fuel economic development.

Mental Well-being

With a heightened awareness of its impact in workplaces, corporate culture now shines a spotlight on mental health. Organizations now invest in employee well-being by offering flexible arrangements and robust support systems. The statistics speak volumes, with one in three American adults and half of all young adults reporting mental health challenges.

Social Media and Sophisticated Misinformation

The rise of social media has positives and negatives. We have transformed interpersonal communications, but subjected ourselves to information overload and the potential for massive amounts of disinformation (false information) and misinformation (facts packaged to deceive). Deciphering the constant stream of updates and notifications is challenging. It hinders productivity and strains mental well-being. Many people experience anxiety, stress, and decision paralysis due to the amount of data bombarding them daily.[9]

Cyber Risks and Privacy Issues

As our dependency on technology grows, so does the need to protect against cyber threats and safeguard personal privacy. Cybersecurity is of paramount concern in our interconnected world, demanding stringent protection measures and comprehensive privacy policies.

The traditional paradigms that once guided us fade as technology advances, demographics shift, and global challenges become more complex. When conditions are stable, we do not challenge operating models. People work in the same roles for years. When small disruptions occur, middle managers and their teams can often keep the organization progressing smoothly with minimal stress. In other words, the organization can be led from the middle.

This works well sometimes, but what happens when complex disruptions explode together? That's the time for true leaders to step up to the plate, and step up they must. With so many moving parts, governments and private or public organizations cannot stand still. No organization can ignore these challenges. To do so is to court disaster. Leaders must embrace ambiguity, challenge conventions, and foster connections with diverse minds. Adaptability is key. With unwavering conviction, these leaders will not only weather the storms of disruption but seize them as opportunities for growth. They will pave a path to a

---

[9] Nirmita Panchal, Heather Saunders, Robin Rudowitz & Cynthia Cox, "The Implications of COVID-19 for Mental Health and Substance Use," *KFF.org*. San Francisco: KFF, 20 March 2023. https://www.kff.org/mental-health/issue-brief/the-implications-of-covid-19-for-mental-health-and-substance-use/, accessed 28 December 2023.

future of brilliant, limitless potential. In this era of profound disruption, leadership must undergo a radical transformation.

Now, armed with the knowledge of these disruptive forces, let us explore what type of leadership we need. Adapting to these changes and leading with wisdom is now more crucial than ever.

Buckle up, for this journey will unveil the extraordinary challenges and incredible opportunities for leadership transformation that lie ahead.

Inadequacy of Current Leadership Models

You cannot talk about leadership success without acknowledging failures. An outstandingly successful manager can be a bad leader. This depends entirely on how you define success.

Financial success in a company, for example, means ensuring a steady flow of profit, strong, efficient balance sheets, delivering earnings per share and share price growth above expectations, and increasing share prices. While all these are legitimate measures of success, these do not mean the executives and managers are good leaders. Sometimes, expanding markets make leaders look good; as those leaders say, "rising tides lift all boats." Even so, how you obtained those successes and what you do with them says a lot more about your leadership skills.

Over the past generation, America has been debating managerial accomplishments versus leadership success. As a result, you see executives with private jets, vacation homes, and "golden parachute" retirement plans, making eighty or a hundred times the salary of the lowest-paid employees. Some of them get rid of people right, left, and center without any conscience or cause while hiring and firing on a whim. They treat individuals like commodities, all in the name of short-term returns for the shareholders and bonuses for themselves. Some played fast and loose with the rules and ended up in jail.

None of these are leadership. It's management—management at its worst. They got the job done, doing whatever was needed to get it done. (Scary thought, isn't it?)

I've also worked with executives who were good managers with high moral values, but they weren't good examples of how to drive success, motivate people, or commit to the greater good. They paid people fairly, valued and mentored employees, never dismissed employees without cause, refused the outward excesses of success, and retired to spend their golden years donating time and money to good causes. They got the job done and did it right.

Now, a good, by-the-book manager can also be a good leader, but it does not happen automatically because they are simply not the same thing. Good managers deliver positive results. Good leaders empower and enable people.

People often mistake good management for good leadership because they don't know the difference. However, there is a clear distinction between the two: Management primarily focuses on achieving set results, while leadership revolves around improving people's lives. True leaders navigate complex and ambiguous situations, effectively influencing individuals to collaborate toward shared goals.

As we tackle the new leadership requirements highlighted by disruptive challenges, it's crucial to acknowledge the limitations of our existing models. By acknowledging these shortcomings, we can nurture growth and enhance our approach to leadership.

Short-term thinking is the societal disease of our time.

−Warren Bennis[10]

---

[10] Warren Bennis, *On Becoming a Leader*. New York: Addison Wesley, 1989.

So now let us explore some key areas that require attention in today's leadership:

Lack of Vision

Effective leadership hinges on a clear and inspiring vision. Too many leadership approaches fall short by not emphasizing the importance of vision. They devote most of their attention to managing processes and neglect the acquisition of knowledge and insights. This limits the development of competence and expertise, which are crucial elements for achieving a vision. Often, leaders incorporate vision statements in business plans without embodying that vision in their daily actions. Without a compelling and integrated vision, it's difficult for leaders to align their teams and navigate challenges with purpose and direction. Many leaders struggle to communicate a compelling vision because they lack one for themselves. Consequently, they resort to being taskmasters and fail to create a positive, engaging work environment that fosters innovation, creativity, and commitment. The vision must not be constantly tailored to daily needs, and it must be an over-arching insight into what might be someday—a future that transcends short-term global events.

Finite Mindset

Leaders who lean heavily on a finite mindset are rooted in past successes, including their established methods and personal experiences. They stubbornly resist acknowledging changes in technology, the economy, industry, politics, or any other global shifts that demand business transformation. They impede the flow of innovative ideas and become obstacles to anything that challenges the *status quo*. Fixed in their beliefs, they staunchly refuse to evolve alongside an evolving world.

Ethical Challenges

Authentic leadership finds its foundation in core values and ethical conduct. Too many leaders deviate from their values in pursuit of short-term gains. Compromise erodes trust and undermines the essence of effective leadership. Common ethical challenges include a lack of transparency, conflicts of interest driven by personal gain, abuse of authority that leads to harassment or discrimination, biased accountability standards, and the failure to foster a safe, non-political environment. Preserving the highest personal standards and integrity remains a concern for high-profile leaders.

Hindrance to Innovation

Disruptive challenges call for leaders who can create a culture that encourages thinking outside the box and fosters innovation. Traditional models often prioritize conformity to established norms, which stifles creativity and impedes adaptation to new circumstances. Leaders must understand that challenges faced by their clients and stakeholders demand innovative thinking to solve new problems.

Empathy Deficiency

COVID unleashed unparalleled trauma and anxiety, profoundly impacting people's daily lives. That period made it more obvious that leaders must connect with their teams to understand their people's challenges. Leaders must actively listen to team members, genuinely value their input, and engage with empathy. Leaders need to actively listen to team members–to understand a team member's situation and problem so they can assist in finding solutions.

Trust and Delegation Barrier

Successful leaders comprehend the importance of trust and delegation. They empower their teams, delegate responsibilities, and create a culture of collaboration. Conversely, some leaders struggle to trust team members, leading to micromanagement and limited growth opportunities. Authoritarian leadership styles are still highly prevalent in many organizations. A business leader needs to trust their people and delegate authority while verifying that things are happening as expected. Often, the past impacts a leader's approach, and their lack of trust can come from failures when those they trusted failed. It can be difficult for people to learn from their past failures while not overcompensating. Trust empowers people and can be transformational for businesses.

People Disconnection

Leadership surpasses mere authority. It involves building meaningful relationships with team members. Leaders who exhibit care and empathy and foster a positive work environment cultivate loyalty and dedication among their teams. Leaders who lack a genuine connection to others prioritize their own opinions, fail to empathize, and don't create inclusive environments that embrace diverse perspectives. They often hesitate to form close relationships with team members because of a fear it may hinder their effectiveness. Good communication plays a vital role in establishing empathy and connection. Leaders need to talk to their people as people about more than work. Those who fail to build genuine connections with team members will struggle to succeed.

Hierarchical Constraints

The conventional top-down approach restricts the flow of ideas and inhibits innovation and responsiveness in a rapidly changing environment. The outdated command-and-control leadership style stifles creativity, discourages risk-taking, and restricts autonomy. In today's disruptive landscape, leaders must empower and inspire by embracing input from all levels of the organization and fostering an open and collaborative culture.

Inflexibility

Conventional models prioritize stability and consistency over adaptability. Today's business environment isn't stable, so leaders must be ready to pivot as needed. They must make informed decisions in times of uncertainty and quickly adjust strategies when needed. Many existing models are risk-averse, which impedes embracing and navigating disruptive forces. Inflexible leaders cannot effectively manage change because they do not have the right mindset to perform in the new normal of our world.

Self-Gain

While individual leadership is crucial, disruptive challenges often require collective efforts. Leaders must facilitate cross-functional teamwork and foster diversity and inclusion. Current leadership models may not adequately address the necessity of collaboration, focusing instead on their personal agendas and the individual needs of senior leaders instead of the needs of the whole team or the entire organization.

I will not confess to making every mistake on this (not all-inclusive) list, but I do admit to making enough of them to speak with some authority on the subject.

Disruptive Leadership—What Is It?

It's not the critic who counts, not the man who points out how the strong man stumbles or where the doer of deeds could have done better. The credit belongs to the man who is actually in the arena, whose face is marred by dust and sweat and blood, who strives valiantly, who errs and comes up short again and again, because there is no effort without error or shortcoming, but who knows the great enthusiasms, the great devotions, who spends himself in a worthy cause; who, at best, knows, in the end, the triumph of high achievement, and who, at the worst, if he fails, at least he fails while daring greatly, so that his place shall never be with those cold and timid souls who knew neither victory nor defeat.

—Theodore Roosevelt (italics are mine)[11]

---

[11] Theodore Roosevelt, "Citizenship in a Republic." Speech at the Sorbonne, Paris, April 23, 1910. Read the complete text at: https://www.worldfuturefund.org/Documents/maninarena.htm, accessed 21 February 2024.

My Point of View

Certain characteristics can be found among truly disruptive leaders:

They possess an unwavering determination to overcome obstacles hindering the achievement of their audacious goals. These individuals possess a mindset outlining how tasks should be executed. They also remain open to navigating reality, adapting their approach for optimal results. Endowed with remarkable resilience, their unwavering pursuit of their envisioned success eclipses any hardships they encounter along the way.

They also embrace a panoramic perspective, encompassing both the broad strokes of the big picture and the intricate nuances of other levels. They enjoy the rare ability to synthesize diverse viewpoints from varied sources, seamlessly blending creativity, systematic thinking, and practicality. When accomplishing this delicate balance, they exude both assertiveness and open-mindedness.

However, their defining attribute lies in an inexhaustible passion for their endeavors. These leaders are driven by an unwavering commitment to excellence, manifesting an intolerance toward mediocrity in those who work alongside them. Above all, they hold a profound desire to leave an indelible and positive impact on the world.

Disruptive leadership is not a style of management. It's a philosophy that transcends conventional boundaries, propelling us toward a future of profound progress for a higher purpose. At its core, disruptive leadership dares to challenge the norms and conventions that confine us, serving as a catalyst for extraordinary change. It rejects complacency and embraces innovation. It allows leaders to take calculated risks in pursuit of transformation and growth for the greater good.

I believe that to be a disruptive leader is to reject settling for small, incremental improvements. It's a constant quest for betterment, not just for yourself as a leader, but for the organization, the community, and the world. An insatiable hunger for improvement drives disruptive leaders as they relentlessly seek new ways to do business, serve employees, and delight clients. They embrace complexity, see change as an opportunity, and lead from the front, inspiring others to challenge the rules and pursue breakthrough ideas.

By the way, you don't have to change the whole world. For many disruptive leaders, their vision will simply change one small corner of the world. If that's enough for them, it's enough.

Disruptive leades are contrarians, unafraid of dissenting from conventional wisdom in pursuit of the greater good:

- They challenge established norms and outdated practices and influence others to change these even in tough situations.
- They thrive on risk-taking, not being traditional thinkers, and use creative problem-solving to tackle significant obstacles rather than settling for small victories.
- They learn voraciously, continuously gathering insights from diverse sources to inspire innovation.
- They show resilience in extreme adversity because their higher purpose gives them strength.

A disruptive leader's transformation begins from within. They understand that personal growth and self-improvement are prerequisites for creating meaningful change in others and across the world.

Disruptive leaders do not rest on their laurels when things go well. They hold themselves to a high standard, constantly pushing their boundaries and grappling with their own biases and limitations. They continually evolve, which sets an example for others to embrace the power of transformation.

In a world where technology unveils new possibilities at an exponential pace, a disruptive leader must grasp the impact of these possibilities on their organization. By embracing technological innovations, they harness its potential to address existing and emerging challenges. However, they always prioritize the human aspect, ensuring that the human needs of their employees and stakeholders outweigh all other considerations.

Disruptive leaders have entrepreneurial spirits and possess a deep-rooted desire to build something new. They have a mindset that drives calculated, purposeful risk-taking rather than risk aversion. Challenging the status quo and hierarchical structures comes naturally, and they consistently operate in a creative, proactive mode rather than with a compliance attitude. Disruptive leaders work collaboratively to drive new ideas and innovative approaches to shape the future. They have the humility to hire people who are smarter than they are. To embrace disruptive leadership, we must recognize the seven key principles that underpin its realization:

1. Develop a disruptive mindset.
2. Find a disruptive higher purpose.
3. Get outside your comfort zone and overcome your inertia.
4. Build relationships that foster disruptive thinking.
5. Disrupt the status quo.
6. Conquer complacency and mental fragility.
7. Disrupt what accountability means and why results matter.

Disruptive leadership does not disrupt for the sake of being different or unconventional. It's not about being a contrarian or going against the grain to gain notoriety. It's not synonymous with being authoritarian or autocratic. It doesn't impose ideas or decisions without involving others and considering their input.

Disruptive leadership does not

- create unnecessary chaos or confusion within an organization;
- disregard established norms, rules, or processes without justification;
- make impulsive or reckless decisions;

- promote a culture of conflict or disunity within a team or organization;
- take unnecessary risks;
- ignore commitments and obligations to stakeholders;
- impose change or disruption for the sake of change;
- undermine the stability and functionality of an organization;
- disrespect or alienate others in any position; and
- neglect the business results and growth of the organization.

Disruptive leadership is not exclusive to certain industries or sectors. While it's often associated with innovation-driven fields, such as technology or startups, it's relevant and can benefit numerous industries and business sectors. It's a continuous process, an evolution that embraces change to drive meaningful progress and growth rather than a single event or action.

For those who dare to embrace disruptive leadership, the power to influence the course of a changing world lies within their grasp. This is important if we are to solve the new, emerging challenges. Some problems are technological (advancing digital capabilities and AI), some are societal (changing work-life expectations and the ethnic composition of populations), some are political (climate change and corruption), and some are individual (increased remote employment and entrepreneurship). All those changes will, ultimately, affect much, if not all, of what we do and how we do it in the future.

What is "the next big thing" that will change our lives for better or worse? How do we deal with the disruptions that change will cause? What about the environmental or societal disruptions our own work may cause?

In the modern world, all these questions stare us in the face and demand answers. The answers are simple, in theory, though not so easy in practice:

- Do not wait for disruption; enable it.

- You cannot always control change—market change, business change, climate change, political and geopolitical change, monetary policy change, family and personal circumstances change—but you can change how you deal with those situations.
- You cannot do it alone. You need a network of disruptive individuals and companies to support you.
- You will meet resistance. You must be ready to deal with different opinions and be able to demonstrate how your way is better.
- Change does not always happen quickly. You need to embrace the long view and careful planning as cornerstones.
- Those who live for the status quo will fight you. Be prepared for some unpleasant consequences.

With all this in mind, if you are up for the challenge, you can be one of those who trims the sails and changes the course of "the next big thing."

Leadership Is Not a Joy Ride

Leaders get people moving. They energize and mobilize. They take people and organizations to places they have never been before. Leadership is not a fad, and the leadership challenge never goes away. In uncertain and turbulent times, accepting that challenge is the only antidote to chaos, stagnation, and disintegration. Times change, problems change, technologies change, and people change. Leadership endures. Teams, organizations, and communities need people to step up and take charge.

—James Kouzes and Barry Posner[12]

---

[12] James Kouzes & Barry Posner, *The Leadership Challenge: How to Make Extraordinary Things Happen in Organizations*, 7th edition. Hoboken, NJ: Jossey-Bass, an imprint of Wiley, Inc.; 2023.

One final note before we get into the practicalities of the subject: Leadership is a journey where people regularly go through tough times, times that allow them to become better leaders and better people.

An old sage once joked, "If you're going to sit in the center seat, you'll have to put up with some lumps in the cushion."

Throughout my diverse leadership experiences, I have been fortunate to witness extraordinary transformations in individuals. Initially met with skepticism, disagreement, and resistance to change, these individuals gradually embraced wise counsel and ultimately blossomed into devoted followers.

As a manager, you can follow a more standard approach to work and ensure adherence and compliance with agreed plans and rules of the organization. As a leader, life becomes more intricate. It's through complexity that we discover the lessons we need to learn. Management revolves around meeting someone else's expectations, while leadership involves choosing and establishing our own expectations. Leaders compete with themselves to improve every day.

Managers, with their rational and task-oriented approach, certainly play a crucial role in organizational functioning. However, true leadership transcends mere managerial skills and delves into the realm of heartfelt commitment. Amidst the multitude of factors that sustain leaders on their arduous journey, love emerges as an enduring force. It's unfathomable to envision leaders rising each day, dedicating countless hours and unwavering effort to achieve extraordinary results without wholeheartedly investing their emotions. The elusive key to the triumphs of prosperous leaders lies in their unwavering love, a perpetual zeal for leading, for the tireless contributions of individuals, for the profound impact their organizations generate, and for those who honor the organization by embracing its offerings. Leadership cannot be reduced to logical reasoning alone; it's an affair that originates from the profound depths of the heart.

Embracing leadership challenges empowers us to navigate uncharted territories, foster growth, and inspire those around us to exceed their own limitations. Each encounter becomes an opportunity for personal and collective growth, shaping a future filled with endless possibilities. The disruptive mindset can benefit a wide range of leaders, including the following:

- **Corporate Leaders.** In today's highly competitive business landscape, disruptive thinking helps organizations stay ahead of the curve. This book demonstrates how corporate leaders can foster a culture of innovation, encourage risk-taking, and drive transformation within their organizations.
- **Entrepreneurs.** New venture leaders navigate uncertainty and rapidly changing environments as a matter of course. This book presents strategies to help keep them thinking differently, continually challenge the status quo, and embrace radical methods of achievement.
- **Team Leaders.** By encouraging creative problem-solving, helping team members to challenge conventional wisdom, and fostering an environment that embraces change, team leaders can inspire team members to overcome obstacles with new methods and drive positive change within the team.
- **Nonprofit Leaders.** Like any other industry, nonprofits face challenges and need to adapt to changing landscapes. This book provides insights into how to disrupt traditional approaches, engage differently with stakeholders, and find innovative solutions to effectively address social issues.
- **Government and Public Sector Leaders.** Public sector leaders operate within complex bureaucratic systems that seem to thrive on the status quo. Disruptive leadership can help them challenge traditional norms, find innovative solutions to societal problems, and drive meaningful change within government or public sector organizations.

Remember: *The leadership journey never ends!*

CHAPTER 2

Developing the Disruptive Mindset

As I reflect upon my thirty-year professional journey, I recognize the immense value of embracing a different way of thinking and approaching challenges. Time and again, I witness people adhering to unspoken rules that confine them. However, it always troubled me that these rules were established in a different era, tailored to suit those times.

Today, we have to move our businesses much faster, so our organizations need to question and challenge the "norms" to meet the changing dynamics of current and future generations.

From my very first role as a trainee systems analyst, I felt compelled to challenge the status quo. I just couldn't understand why most people around me were happy to conform and do things the same way over and over. I think this attitude comes from my parents' guidance—to use my mind and always try to do better, as well as to avoid the boredom of repetition. The ability to break free from the limitations imposed by traditional thinking has not only empowered me but also fueled my endeavors to build successful enterprises. This daring mindset has become an integral part of who I am, shaping the person I am today. When I am not thinking differently, I feel stagnant. Thinking differently, acting differently, and often respectfully defying conventions motivates me and has benefited both me and my stakeholders, including employers, investors, clients, partners, and even family members, who have valued my abilities in this space over the years.

Cultivating the disruptive mindset goes beyond personal gain. It means forging a better future for others. By challenge the status quo, disruptive leaders attempt to create opportunities that transcend boundaries and unlock potential. It's a journey they undertake with the utmost passion and a deep-seated desire to leave a positive impact on the world.

Watch your thoughts; they become words. Watch your words; they become actions. Watch your actions; they become habits. Watch your habits; they become character. Watch your character; it becomes your destiny.

—Attributed to Gautama Buddha, Lao Tzu, and others[13]

Our Mindset Creates Infinite Opportunities

When you put everything you have into pursuing your dreams, they manifest. In the journey toward shifting our mindset, we must choose to embrace the certainty of a VUCA world—a constantly volatile, uncertain, complex, and ambiguous reality, rather than clinging to preconceived notions of how things should be. Individual perspectives shape the way we perceive the world, but it's crucial to acknowledge that we are sometimes wrong. By denying the existence of new problems, we hinder the ability to find solutions.

To foster growth and evolution, we must remain open to different perspectives and challenge ingrained beliefs. This requires a deep sense of self-awareness, as we must be willing to reflect on our own thinking patterns and biases. My experiences helped me to realize I sometimes deny a contradicting alternative view at first pass, but I've learned to question myself and now understand the importance of always questioning and setting aside my preconceived ideas and self-imposed limitations.

The brain begins to wire itself with intricate connections as billions of neurons connect early in life. According to Carl

---

[13] The earliest known expression of this idea is found in Indian Vedic literature, written sometime between 1500 and 900 BC.

Zimmer,[14] the brain comprises close to 100 billion neurons, each with as many as 1,000 connections in different parts of the brain. That creates at least 100 trillion neural links. These connections form the foundation of our thoughts, skills, and abilities. As we navigate the world, our mental conditioning and wiring shape our perception of reality. I refer to this as "programming" the brain, and this has both positive and negative implications, depending on your mindset and how you view the world. The stories and thoughts we believe in or share with others are directly influenced by our neural networks and the memories they create.

Embracing the power of self-reflection and actively challenging our mental programming opens us up to new possibilities and transformative experiences. It's through conscious effort to break free from our mental constraints that we can uncover new ways of thinking, problem-solving, and living a more fulfilling life.

My journey began in India, where societal conditioning ran deep and dictated the path of many. I was enveloped by self-limiting beliefs ingrained in my mind as I grew up. The idea of slowly climbing the corporate ladder to reach the top just before retirement was the accepted narrative. The influence of British bureaucracy, with its top-down mentality, had left a lasting mark on the collective consciousness.

I witnessed the manifestation of these beliefs, watching my father's career trajectory. Starting as a civil engineer, he eventually ascended to a directorial position in a government organization. Slow and steady was the name of the game. I admired my father's accomplishments and his courage to leave his village for opportunities completely outside his comfort zone. He played a critical role in helping build essential infrastructure, such as railways, working in large public-sector organizations. His version of a transformational mindset was to

---

[14] Carl Zimmer, "100 Trillion Connections: New Efforts Probe and Map the Brain's Detailed Architecture," *ScientificAmerican.com*. Berlin, Germany: Springer Nature, 1 January 2011. https://www.scientificamerican.com/article/100-trillion-connections/, accessed 2 January 2024.

earn respect from the international community and prove that India is self-sufficient in key infrastructure development. He had to conform to the standards and bureaucratic structures that India inherited from the British. I could not help but feel the weight of conformity pressing upon me. However, fate intervened when I ventured to Australia in my early twenties. The land Down Under offered a fresh perspective on life's challenges and opportunities. An egalitarian spirit prevailed, emphasizing the importance of skills over experience and granting everyone a "fair go." Age did not automatically confer wisdom or expertise.

This shift in environment fueled my ambition and infinite mindset, awakening a sense of self-awareness and the realization that I could challenge the status quo, unlike in my birth country. I embarked on a journey of disruptive thinking, constantly questioning and seeking unconventional solutions.

Acquiring a master's degree bolstered my confidence and prepared me to enter the workforce. I hoped that if I showcased my skills and proved my effectiveness, then any job would be within my reach. With this more confident mindset, I secured my first full-time job as the information systems manager for St. Andrews Hospital Group and quickly moved to become the director of corporate services in Rockhampton at the young age of twenty-five.

Determined to keep pushing the boundaries, I pursued opportunities with the Queensland Public Service in Brisbane. I joined Queensland Health and continued to aggressively pursue my plans to advance my career. There were many setbacks and rejections as I aimed for senior executive roles. Nevertheless, I refused to let these obstacles define me. I knew I had the necessary skills to become a chief information officer (CIO), so I persevered.

At twenty-nine, I achieved what others deemed improbable. I became CIO and director of information management for the Queensland Department of Tourism, Sport, and Racing. I proudly held the title of the youngest CIO in the Queensland government. Despite peers who were decades older, my unique mindset, drive, and unwavering focus propelled me forward. Recognition arrived in the form of the Premier's Leadership Excellence Award for my contributions to the government in 2000.

So, how did the shy kid from India reach an executive role in a conservative Australian region at twenty-nine?

I differentiated myself from other candidates. I could see the organizations were struggling with the changes they needed to make, so I had to find a way to drive change. This meant reprograming my thoughts, rewiring my neural networks, and challenging self-imposed limitations. I cast aside the shackles of conformity and embraced a mindset that sought new possibilities, always creating value for stakeholders. Reflection, self-exploration, and a relentless pursuit of personal growth became my guiding principles.

As my perspective expanded, so did the opportunities that lay before me. Thus, through the power of mental metamorphosis, I defied the norm and blazed a trail to manifest my grand aspirations to serve others.

In personal journeys, we will inevitably encounter individuals, sometimes quite powerful and influential, who cast doubt upon both our capabilities and the dreams we cherish. These doubters adamantly proclaim that our aspirations are unattainable, lacking faith in our abilities or dismissing the possibility altogether. As we strive for greater heights for the benefit of others, the frequency of meeting such nonbelievers tends to increase. Throughout history, remarkable artists and creative minds have crossed paths with these skeptics, individuals who fail to comprehend the essence of ambitious dreams. This phenomenon extends to the realm of business as well. I faced opposition from many in the early stages who were determined to prove me wrong and, in some instances, even actively tried to terminate the projects.

Nonetheless, amidst the odds stacked against us, all disruptive leaders share one resolute trait: unwavering persistence in the face of skepticism and doubt. They often get energized by naysayers. They are an inescapable part of life's journey that many like us have experienced all our lives. However, I know their influence and authority over the paths we choose to take are merely illusory. These individuals find themselves uncomfortably out of their depth, apprehensive about venturing into the unknown, and unaccustomed to taking risks beyond their comfort zones. They have never possessed the strength required to pursue endeavors comparable to the one we are currently embarking upon. They lack the courage to craft a bold life vision and wholeheartedly dedicate themselves to its realization. This allows us to dare to

- dream big;
- build high-impact relationships;
- drive bold transformational change;
- take calculated risks and manage them;
- differentiate ourselves and not follow the crowd; and
- communicate with respectful radical candor.

Dare to Dream Big

Do not go where the path may lead, go instead where there is no path and leave a trail.

–Attributed to Ralph Waldo Emerson[15]

Only leaders who dare to dream big can revolutionize industries, push boundaries, and transform the world.

Dreaming on a grand scale fuels innovation and progress. By embracing audacious dreams that surpass feasibility or reality, disruptive leaders open doors to new possibilities.

---

[15] Commonly attributed to Emerson, the quote is not known among his writings. A very similar statement, "I will not follow where the path may lead, but I will go where there is no path, and I will leave a trail," is found in "Wind-Wafted Wild Flowers," a poem by Muriel Strode, published August 1903. Read the poem at: https://www.tumblr.com/missedstations/90051688935/wind-wafted-wild-flowers-muriel-strode, accessed 28 December 2023.

They challenge themselves and their teams to think outside the box, question existing norms, and explore unconventional paths. This mindset cultivates creativity and encourages the exploration of uncharted territories.

Dreaming big also sparks passion and motivation. When innovative leaders set their sights on ambitious visions, they inspire and rally their teams toward a common purpose. The pursuit of a big dream energizes individuals and gives them a sense of purpose and a shared drive to overcome obstacles. It fosters a sense of belonging, unifying everyone around a compelling mission, and amplifies collaboration and collective effort.

The ability to communicate that big dream helps attract and retain top talent. Ambitious individuals are drawn to visionary leaders who take risks and pursue large-scale goals. Those who embrace big dreams have a magnetic appeal, attracting like-minded individuals who are equally passionate and eager to make a difference. These talented people are not simply seeking employment; they also yearn for an opportunity to be part of something extraordinary and leave their mark on the world.

In complex missions, big dreams also instill resilience and determination. Forward-thinking leaders understand that the journey toward achieving audacious goals has many challenges. However, by creating a powerful shared vision, leaders fortify themselves and their teams with unwavering belief in their abilities to overcome obstacles and persevere in the face of adversity. The determination to manifest big dreams grants them the strength to weather challenges and setbacks, allowing them to grow stronger along the way.

For most of my formative years, I lacked dreams and ambitions. I navigated the education system diligently, striving to excel in my studies, but without any particular passion or goal driving me. Thanks to my mother's steadfast discipline and guidance, I achieved good grades in high school. This success led me to pursue economics at the prestigious Birla Institute of Technology and Science in India.

Although my interest in economics was lackluster, a spark of curiosity ignited within me during my first two years of college—I found a passion for philosophy. Immersing myself in countless books, I explored the depths of thought and the power of the human mind. I developed a resolute belief that one's thoughts and actions hold the key to shaping the future.

With this newfound conviction, I made a daring decision to dream big and strive for the perfection of getting 10/10 for my last four semesters after merely crossing the pass mark in my first four. Convinced of my abilities, I had an unyielding faith that nothing could stand in my way. Gradually, my grades began to shift, rising to a respectable level and eventually reaching astonishing heights. I did achieve that 10/10 in the last two semesters. This remarkable, at one time unthinkable, result left me bewildered, yet enlightened, granting me a profound realization about the power of dreaming big.

This existential awakening brought about remarkable changes within me. Positivity and enthusiasm radiated, infusing every aspect of my life. I shifted my focus from thinking small to embracing a grander perspective on the possibilities before me. Motivated and inspired, I began making concrete plans and working toward my goals. Even in the face of failure, I remained steadfast, learning from each setback.

Dreaming big has been the cornerstone of my professional journey, propelling me toward incredible achievements. One moment stands out vividly in my memory—the day I met Edge Zarrella, the global managing partner of technology consulting for KPMG. Edge possessed a brilliant aura and a contagious passion for pushing boundaries. During our meeting, he unexpectedly invited me to join his team as the global chief operating officer, uniting our shared belief in dreaming big. Alongside visionary leaders—like Steve Hasty, the US leader; Rob Fijneman, the EMEA leader; and Pradeep Udhas, the Indian leader—we embarked on an audacious mission to transform the technology consulting business into a global powerhouse. Within a decade, its revenue surpassed ten times what it was when we began. We created a multibillion-dollar professional services business that had more than twelve thousand partners and employees when I retired from the firm in 2015.

Fueled by unwavering determination, we faced challenges head-on, innovating at every turn. Though obstacles appeared along the way, our commitment to that lofty dream propelled us forward to think big about creating a multibillion-dollar business. Each step expanded our horizons, and we never allowed our ambition to waver. As the years flew by, the dream we passionately nurtured became a reality—a moment of immense pride and satisfaction. And while some of us moved on to new ventures, the spirit of that big dream lived on, inspiring continued growth and success within the organization.

More than just a leader, Edge was a beacon of inspiration. He taught us to dream not just big but also ten times bigger and on a global scale. His unwavering faith in our collective abilities pushed us beyond self-imposed limitations. Even today, his relentless pursuit of excellence continues to inspire countless individuals, igniting their own dreams and propelling them toward extraordinary achievements.

The Power of Dreaming Big

It's in these audacious ambitions that true change lies. The story of GHD Digital, a testament to the incredible possibilities that lie within the realms of imagination.

With a vision to revolutionize the $200-billion architecture, engineering, and construction (AEC) industry, GHD set out to create a digital business like no other—what became GHD Digital. We aimed to carve a path to unparalleled success. Today, we stand tall as a shining example of what is possible when dreams merge with action.

In a mere five years, GHD Digital rose to become one of the top global digital agencies. With a strong presence in nine countries and a staggering eighty-six offices, we wove a web of innovation and excellence that stretches far and wide. As we were building our digital business, our competitors, some of them the biggest players in the industry, spent billions of dollars to acquire large consulting businesses. We built a similar business organically from the ground up for a fraction of the cost. In January 2024, independent analysts rated us as the industry leader in digital transformation. Our impact is felt, recognized, and celebrated.

So, let us ask ourselves: can this dream be translated into reality?

The resounding answer is an emphatic yes! By remaining steadfast in pursuit of excellence, we propelled ourselves toward the summit of success. Our journey is still just beginning, but it is a testament to the extraordinary heights a passionate and visionary team can reach. That passionate team included everyone—GHD's board, executives, and an incredible group of employees.

Let the story of GHD Digital inspire you to nurture your dreams, for within them lies the power to transform industries, touch lives, and build legacies. As we gaze into the future, never forget that the possibility of achieving greatness rests in your hands. Dream big, pursue relentlessly, and watch as the unimaginable becomes your new reality.

So the legacy of that big dream lives on, reminding us of the power of daring, embracing, and refusing to settle. It serves as a testament that when we dream big, we can achieve incredible feats and leave an indelible mark on the world.

Since that period, dreaming big has been intricately woven into my way of life. Ambitious and audacious goals push me to surpass the boundaries of what I once believed possible. They give me purpose and meaning and allow me to make significant contributions to the world. Pursuing my dreams gives me unparalleled fulfillment and satisfaction.

Ultimately, visionary leaders have the potential to create a lasting legacy. They become catalysts for change and drive progress, not just within their organizations but within entire industries and societies. By setting their sights on a future that surpasses current limitations, they leave the world a better place.

I urge you to nurture the courage to dream big. Embrace the unknown, shatter the limitations that confine you, and dare to envision a future that surpasses "reasonable" expectations. For within the realms of outlandish dreams lies the potential to unlock your fullest capabilities.

Dare to Build High-Impact Relationships

Disruptive leaders prioritize building high-impact relationships because it's rare to achieve success in isolation. By cultivating strong connections with like-minded individuals, influential stakeholders, and industry experts, leaders can accelerate their growth, drive innovation, and amplify their impact.

My experiences and rewiring at the start of my career in Queensland, Australia, taught me the true value of building relationships with key leaders. And this lesson became another cornerstone of my journey. Over the next two decades, meeting prime ministers, premiers, federal and state ministers, CEOs, billionaires, community leaders, movie stars, and countless other influential men and women (considered leaders in their fields), I carefully nurtured every connection, forming relationships and networks.

In the present age, high-impact relationships encompass more than just influential leaders. They encompass the collective of talented young professionals, innovative entrepreneurs, forward-thinking community leaders, visionary artists, and others who possess the ability to approach challenges from unique angles. These individuals, who think differently and bring diverse perspectives to the table, hold the key to solving emerging challenges and shaping a better future. By fostering and nurturing these relationships, we open ourselves to a world of possibilities and ensure that we are well-equipped to tackle the complexities and uncertainties that lie ahead.

Working at KPMG for almost half of my professional life bestowed upon me the rare privilege of collaborating closely with influential leaders in a large business ecosystem. They often became my sponsors. From the global chairman, the late Michael Andrew, to chairmen and CEOs of various country practices and global, regional, and national leaders, each interaction left a permanent impression on my life. These partnerships forged true friendships with senior leaders such as Edge Zarrella, Steve Hasty, Pradeep Udhas, and Ian Hancock. They not only guided and mentored me but also entrusted me with leading significant parts of the business—a responsibility I cherish to this day. I equally cherish the strong relationships I was fortunate to build at GHD over the last few years with esteemed leaders at all levels, from young professionals to technical experts and executive leaders, both internally and externally, who supported and enabled me to achieve my higher purpose of leading the creation of a global business. At GHD Digital, our triumphs are indebted to an extraordinary blend of creative geniuses. Our team comprises not only engineers and technologists but also innovators, artists, accountants, scientists, lawyers, and a diverse array of professionals, each contributing their unique experiences and cultural backgrounds to our collective tapestry. It's through their unwavering dedication and synergistic expertise that we have emerged victorious, consistently driving our success forward.

I feel humble and grateful for the relationships cultivated along this extraordinary journey. Each connection contributed to my growth, shaped my perspectives, and inspired me to push beyond the limits. These leaders believed in me and provided the support and opportunities necessary to fulfill my potential.

High-Impact Relationships Offer Access to Diverse Perspectives and Expertise

Successful disruption usually requires a multifaceted approach, a combination of different skill sets and knowledge domains. By actively seeking relationships with people from different backgrounds, industries, and disciplines, disruptive leaders gain access to a wealth of knowledge, fresh perspectives, and innovative ideas that can fuel their creativity and problem-solving abilities.

High-Impact Relationships Often Act as Catalysts for Collaboration and Partnerships

Leaders may possess groundbreaking ideas, but bringing these ideas to life requires collaborative efforts. By building strong relationships with potential collaborators, strategic partners, and investors, leaders can tap into additional resources, shared expertise, and the funding opportunities necessary to scale up their innovations and reach a wider audience.

High-Impact Relationships Are Vital for Disruptive Leaders

Relationships provide support, diverse perspectives, collaborative opportunities, and enhanced credibility. By nurturing relationships, it's possible for leaders to accelerate growth, drive innovation, and make a lasting, positive impact in their respective industries. However, engaging with high-impact leaders cannot be at the cost of genuine interactions with young people who clearly teach us about the expectations of the next generation of customers or those from entirely different industries who can show us different ways to deal with problems. It also does not remove us from the learnings of those who are less fortunate. These leaders help us accelerate what we learn from our broader networks.

I invite you to embrace the power of connections; never underestimate their impact on your journey. Build relationships, learn from the best, and allow their belief in you to propel you toward your own extraordinary achievements.

Why Am I Sharing These Examples?

These incredible relationships enabled the creation of a network of trusted, high-quality leaders who allowed me to fulfill my higher purpose and career/personal goals. My learning was fast-tracked due to these relationships and interactions as I evolved into a better leader.

Dare to Drive Bold, Transformational Change

Disruptive leaders have the responsibility of driving massive change and understand there are ways to do things other than "the way we've always done it."

They need to drive change responsibly, but moving too slowly will compromise their effectiveness. Driving responsible change fast is challenging for many and is a skill that leaders must acquire. Not changing fast enough or delaying key decisions can drive down team morale. I believe that contrary to the common approach of slow-and-steady incremental change, we need to move quickly with clear daily and weekly processes to monitor progress.

The purpose of creating GHD Digital surpassed the mere pursuit of fiscal success. We were united in our endeavor to spearhead a metamorphosis to diversify and better serve our clients within our GHD global enterprise. Our vision expanded beyond financial gains, stretching into the very fabric of our value chain and enriching our integrated offerings to address emerging client issues.

With fervent hope, we aspired to technological changes that would ignite a blazing enthusiasm among other prominent industry players. We still hope our strides in digital transformation serve as inspiration, propelling others toward adopting innovative strategies that elevate not only their own organizational capabilities but also the overall maturity of the industry itself.

Let us embark together on this journey toward creating a profound societal impact, expanding the boundaries of possibility. There are five things most successful disruptive leaders must do to drive change:

They Are Forward Thinking about the Need To Change

Leaders with strong strategic thinking skills recognize the need for change before others can comprehend it. They anticipate the next shift required and move to implement change before others come on board. These leaders can articulate the reasons for change much more clearly as they have worked on the change agenda individually or with a group of people. They can "join the dots" and see connections between unrelated things. They can better enunciate the benefits, motivating their teams to move forward.

Collaboratively Enlist People for the Cause

Leaders who successfully enlist their teams and followers early in the process can move faster and create momentum for action. Early enlistment helps bring diversity of thought and a greater level of ownership. However, leaders must ensure that they enlist the right people with the right skills. Otherwise, the enlistment process can backfire, and the change initiative can stall. Therefore, rather than enlist people based on their title or power base, disruptive leaders should look for those who can have a positive impact, be action-orientated, and move quickly.

Even people who are slow at adopting change can play extremely important roles. They simply need to buy into a different way to operate. An empathic and patient approach is needed to ensure such team members are rightly onboarded. Active listening and responding to people's concerns creates a greater ownership of the initiative. Listening without judgment also helps to garner valuable feedback in areas where the leader may have limited experience. Driving massive changes has many obstacles, and receiving feedback on areas of improvement not only makes people feel valued but also helps refine a path to success.

Communicate Clearly at all Times

We can be the best strategic thinkers who can bring on the right team members, but true change will not happen unless leaders communicate in a meaningful and relatable manner to align their teams. Here, I find optimism and positively articulating a new way of doing things hugely impacts team members' understanding, so they actively contribute to its success.

In complex situations, I believe in overcommunication. I strongly believe that even though change may be complex and challenging, hearing from the leader regularly helps provide assurance and reduces bottled-up feelings that can upset the agenda.

Plan for Quick Wins and Deliver Them

While leaders need to think big and have a bold vision, they should drive execution in an agile manner with quick wins. Adopting a program and project management approach is the best way to get those wins. I ensure our teams adopt a task, project, program, and portfolio approach to planning the change objective so they break it into executable tasks and actions. This allows us to monitor progress daily and helps deliver major milestones. Quick wins are important to maintain the momentum for change.

Change Yourself before You Change Others

When individuals ascend to influential positions, such as chairman, president, managing director, or any C-level or E-level role, they often overlook their personal growth. They may assume that reaching the zenith of success exempts them from further advancement. Sadly, many leaders find themselves inundated, their calendars brimming with meetings and travel, engulfed in a perpetual state of busyness. In their pursuit of countless initiatives, whether consequential or not, these senior figures neglect crucial aspects such as self-reflection, self-awareness, self-care, and self-improvement. As they navigate from one meeting to another, toiling long hours and mistakenly believing they are effecting change, these leaders lose track of external occurrences and developments. Their inflated perspective, reinforced within their limited sphere, where they hold the utmost authority, often leads them to surround themselves with agreeable individuals who comply with their demands and share their narrow worldview.

Disruptive forces that pose a threat to the business may go unnoticed. Leaders may dismiss opposing views and seldom welcome constructive challenges. Such leaders become a detriment to their organizations and society as a whole, failing to grow personally or foster the growth of those they lead. They put not only themselves at risk but also the thousands of employees under their guidance.

Throughout my career, I have, unfortunately, witnessed too many leaders of this kind. They exist in every industry, and some have brought down formerly successful organizations. They are like termites, slowly but steadily weakening the foundations of organizations built over decades. While everything may appear fine and solid on the outside, they become internally weaker and weaker until, one day, they crumble. People are often surprised by these sudden changes, but they should not be if they analyze the leadership within these organizations.

I was fortunate to have worked in two global organizations, KPMG and GHD, where leaders promote self-development and self-awareness. Their cultures fostered open and honest conversations and feedback to those leading the organizations at a senior level without fear of retaliation. Access to excellent mentors and external coaches created an excellent environment for personal and business growth.

There is no doubt that in order to have a truly meaningful impact and effectively lead change, leaders must prioritize their own self-improvement and continuous learning. In truth, all successful business, community, and organizational leaders can also become leaders in life. But they need to work on themselves continuously—no matter what job they have or at what level. My experience showed me that leaders in life need to work on themselves harder than they work on anybody else.

As you change for the better, you are in a better position to lead. In today's world, people do not usually think that way.

They are keen to change the world, but because they have "arrived," they do not see the need to change themselves, resulting in a loss for us all.

Dare to Take Risks

> *The biggest risk is not taking any risk. In a world that's changing, really, the only strategy that is guaranteed to fail is not taking risks.*
>
> —Mark Zuckerberg[16]

Disruptive leaders should embrace risk-taking as an essential component of their journey toward success. By daring to take risks, they open themselves up to new possibilities, opportunities, and breakthroughs.

All the differentiation you can create for yourself will end up useless to you if you take no risks. Any leader who gives up their comfort zone and decides to grasp an uncertain future for themselves and their people takes a significant risk. In my opinion, we do not have that many people who are willing to do that in our large, conventional organizations, where risk-taking is often perceived as career-limiting. However, in these changing times, to be an effective leader, you need to

- try bold ideas;
- embrace uncertainty;
- develop a spirit of adventure;
- venture beyond real or perceived limitations; and
- encourage teams to be bold.

---

[16] From a 29 October 2011 interview at Y Combinator's Startup School in Palo Alto, California. Quoted in Steve Tobak, "Facebook's Mark Zuckerberg—Insights for Entrepreneurs," *CBSNews.com*. New York City: Columbia Broadcasting System, 31 October 2011. https://www.cbsnews.com/news/facebooks-mark-zuckerberg-insights-for-entrepreneurs/, accessed 28 December 2023.

In large, complex organizational environments, leaders often become excessively risk averse. Embracing risks can bring excitement and present new challenges, although such unfamiliar territory can be frightening for those unaccustomed to taking a leap of faith. Modern leaders must have the courage to dream big and take calculated risks as part of their approach. I understand that caution and self-protection may drive some to avoid risks. However, it's important to recognize that these individuals not only jeopardize their success but also hinder the success of those they lead.

By taking calculated risks, leaders foster a culture of creativity and experimentation that encourages unconventional ideas and approaches. This, in turn, can lead to groundbreaking discoveries. Disruptive leaders understand that failure is an inevitable consequence of risk-taking and view it as an opportunity to learn, adapt, and iterate.

Ultimately, this willingness to fail drives progress and fosters growth.

Dare to Differentiate; Do Not Follow the Crowd

Define a Unique Value Proposition

For leaders with my background, their unique value proposition comes from decades of experience in driving positive change for the benefit of thousands by leveraging new innovations and technologies. Their higher purpose, combined with experience and expertise, enables them to build multi-million-dollar businesses. They stand apart from competitors because they can clearly define and communicate their value proposition to drive significant impact. Why does it matter? Unique value propositions allow the following:

- **Competitive Advantage**. It attracts new clients and stakeholders seeking fresh approaches.
- **Talent Attraction and Retention**. It resonates with new talent and helps nurture long-term relationships based on meeting specific needs and desires.

- **Market Disruption.** I can introduce ideas, products, or services that disrupt markets and create new opportunities.
- **Innovation and Adaptability.** It fuels innovation and pushes me to constantly seek new solutions and strategies to stay ahead in a rapidly changing business environment.
- **Investor and Partner Interest.** It helps me attract investors and partners who recognize growth potential and the likelihood of win-win outcomes.

Think Innovatively

Disruptive leaders are known for their ability to challenge the status quo to drive meaningful innovation within organizations and their markets. Innovative thinking does the following:

- **Encourages** creativity that opens up opportunities for breakthrough advancements and unique strategies that can propel organizations forward
- **Challenges** assumptions and traditional ways of doing things, helps understand the barriers holding organizations back, and finds alternative paths to success
- **Cultivates** a culture of experimentation, inspires teams to take risks, allows for new approach experimentation, and encourages learning from failures
- **Embraces** change and adaptability, drives responsiveness to changing circumstances, allows you to anticipate trends, and adapt strategies to proactively stay ahead of the curve
- **Inspires** and motivates others to challenge the status quo, creating an environment where individuals feel empowered to contribute their unique perspectives

Create a Personal Brand Aligned with a Higher Purpose

Once a leader determines how to stand out from the crowd, branding becomes crucial. In any sector—commercial, charitable, or governmental—having more followers directly correlates to having more influence on the world. In today's hyperconnected world, building a personal brand is key to expanding group membership and gaining recognition as a subject matter expert or thought leader in a particular field or arena. Your brand reflects your credibility and authenticity, which is essential for establishing trust among your audience.

I believe that disruptive leaders bear the responsibility of establishing a culture that resonates with values aligned with their higher purpose. The best leaders consistently exemplify behavior that aligns with these principles. It's this harmonious integration that ultimately defines their personal brand. Leveraging your top-level skills and expertise, you develop a unique brand as you ascend as a leader. People come to you for your masterful abilities and seek your guidance on specific matters. In addition, they need to know what you stand for and trust that you will stay steadfast in your beliefs. By demonstrating authenticity and unwavering passion, you establish a brand that people notice and respect.

Another aspect of my brand revolves around a passion for leveraging technology and innovation to transform the way people work and live. Having successfully resolved similar challenges in the past, I can confidently offer solutions that have proven effective for others.

Leaders who possess clearly defined brands can collectively build an organizational brand. As credible individuals come together, their expertise becomes interconnected. This alignment strengthens the organizational brand by providing clarity of beliefs, values, passion, and initiatives to drive change.

Organizations and leaders that have clarity and drive will more easily gain recognition and build a steadily growing base of followers. Unfortunately, some immensely-talented individuals fail to garner a following. This can often be attributed to their inability to build a successful brand, which may reflect their humility, but it makes it harder for people to follow the vision.

Develop Your Unique Story to Inspire Others

As a leader in the professional services and technology industry, I was always aware of the power of innovation and the ability to challenge the status quo, particularly using technology and renewed business models. But amidst the relentless pursuit of progress, it's possible to overlook the importance of developing your compelling story. Through experience, I realized that my story is not just a collection of facts and achievements; it's also the key to connecting with others on a deeper level to inspire and rally them to support my cause. A compelling story humanizes disruptive ideas, making them more relatable and impactful.

If you want to become a high-level leader, develop a compelling story that does the following:

- **Builds Trust and Credibility**. It helps you establish trust and credibility among your team, investors, customers, and stakeholders. When you share your successes, failures, and lessons learned, you create an authentic connection that fosters trust.
- **Inspires Others**. Disruptive leaders are not only visionaries; they are also catalysts for innovation. Your compelling story has the power to inspire others by showcasing your passion, resilience, and unwavering commitment to your cause. When others can see themselves reflected in your story, it motivates them to join your movement.
- **Differentiates Yourself**. In a sea of disruptive ideas and leaders, your compelling story serves as your unique selling proposition. It sets you apart from the competition by highlighting not just what you do but also why you do it. It helps you stand out and attract the right people and opportunities to support your mission.
- **Communicates Your Vision**. Disruptive ideas can be complex and challenging to articulate. A compelling story simplifies these ideas and communicates your vision in a relatable manner through your experiences. It helps you engage and captivate your audience, whether it's your team, investors, or potential partners.

- **Creates a Lasting Impact**. Storytelling has been an integral part of human culture since time immemorial. A compelling story can transcend time and leave a lasting impact. By sharing your journey, the impact you've made, and your future aspirations, you inspire others to push boundaries, dream big, and make a difference.

Take the time to develop and refine your compelling story. Craft it in a way that conveys your passion, purpose, and the positive change you seek to create. Embrace vulnerability, share your triumphs and setbacks, and let your story serve as a beacon of inspiration for all those who have the privilege to hear it.

Communicate with Respectful, Radical Candor

Collaboration of unique, diverse individuals fosters an environment where innovative solutions can flourish. That's a feat that may prove challenging for teams with homogeneous backgrounds. To fully harness the potential of diversity, leaders must cultivate an atmosphere in which team members feel comfortable sharing ideas and viewpoints without fear of repercussions.

Gone are the days of a top-down approach, where a leader's dominance stifles the voices of others and only allows them to speak when given permission. Instead, leaders must embrace a more open-minded stance, inviting team members to challenge assumptions, voice disagreement, and engage in healthy debates even if it causes momentary delays. It's within this environment that innovation and collaboration thrive and propel business plans forward at an accelerated pace.

I believe that effective communication lies at the heart of conveying an organization's purpose and mission while formulating strategies for success. I am an advocate of practicing radical candor, a concept popularized by Kim Scott in *Radical Candor*. This approach emphasizes the importance of providing open opinions and feedback delivered with respect and honesty. Before radical candor can be exercised, it's important to establish a foundation of trust and empathy. In trusted environments, radical candor fosters open communication across teams, corrects misconceptions, and enables collective wisdom to flow freely.

> *Radical candor is the sweet spot between managers who are obnoxiously aggressive on one side and ruinously empathetic on the other. It's about providing guidance, which involves a mix of praise as well as criticism—delivered to produce better results and help employees achieve.*
>
> *–Kim Malone Scott*[17]

However, radical candor only thrives when it operates as a two-way street. It requires managers to refrain from monopolizing discussions and to invite, instead, dissenting opinions. Managers must also provide opportunities for quieter individuals to express their views to ensure that every voice is heard. People will be encouraged to speak with courage if they understand the disruptive leader's thought and decision-making process.

Throughout my professional journey, I engaged senior leaders with radical candor, respectful of their position and the value of their time. Most appreciated my ability to engage with them openly for the benefit of the organization or clients and often sought my advice. I provided insights derived from critical thinking and analysis, offering perspectives they may not have received from others. The more senior the individual is, the more direct the communication is. Some appreciated this approach, some did not, but they all remembered me and, more often than not, extended invitations for further conversations.

---

[17] Kim Scott, *Radical Candor: Fully Revised & Updated Edition: Be a Kick-Ass Boss Without Losing Your Humanity*. New York City: St. Martin's Press, 2019 (updated edition). Quotation from https://kimmalonescott.com/radical-candor, accessed 28 August 2023.

Disruptive leaders, in their pursuit of progress and authenticity, hold the task of exposing and challenging falsehoods. It means promoting a culture of openness and dealing with fakeness, insincerity, or compliance head-on. I'm well-known for fearlessly calling out "bullshit," aligned with an unwavering commitment to truth, preserving integrity, and fostering an environment of transparency. I have consistently applied this principle with boards, executives, clients, employees, politicians, and others. Do it tactfully and respectfully, offending no one. Their actions not only allow for the dismantling of deceit but also pave the way for genuine growth and meaningful change.

On one occasion, I spoke with an Australian federal minister, highlighting reasons why government policies needed changing to benefit the technology sector and professionals. I feared my candor would sever our relationship, but to my surprise, the minister sent their department secretary (effectively the CEO of that organization) to speak with me further. The minister even flew in to meet with me multiple times over succeeding years to discuss matters of national importance. To this day, that minister remains a cherished friend.

Over the past fifteen years, I have been engaged by large corporations in the private and public sectors to review their technology units and provide candid feedback to their CEOs and boards. They sought my guidance not only because they appreciated the honesty of my insights but also because they trusted me to guide them in addressing the challenges I identified. I am known for my "boardroom candor," which is a testament to the fact that radical candor, delivered respectfully, builds trust and fosters authentic relationships. While my radical (respectful) candor has been warmly embraced and appreciated by those with whom I have built long-term relationships, there have been a few leaders who did not quite resonate with this approach, preventing us from establishing a strong bond and achieving our best results.

Life Is a Journey, Not a Destination

The old saying, "Life is a journey, not a destination," carries much truth—that is probably why we keep saying it.

How has my mindset shift enabled my progress? Mostly, I think it's the constantly changing nature of my thoughts. I am always challenging my beliefs and attitudes and the way I see the world. That shifting is not easy. You must proactively challenge childhood conditioning because we are regularly conditioned, or reconditioned, by our environments.

Life is not solely about the destination. For leaders, it is more about the journey itself. Instead of fixating solely on reaching a specific goal or destination, they understand that the true value lies in the experiences, growth, and lessons acquired along the way.

By embracing the perception of life as a journey, disruptive leaders embrace a more flexible and adaptable mindset. They become willing to venture into uncharted territories, adjust course when necessary, and even redefine their goals based on new insights and challenges.

Rather than fixating solely on the end result, they recognize that transformation happens along the way. It's during this expedition that they refine their skills, challenge conventions, push boundaries, explore new passions and experiences, and ultimately leave a profound impact on the world. These leaders treat each destination as significant but just one step in a much greater adventure. They commit to making the most of every step along the way.

Such thinking requires a profound shift beyond the traditional organizational mindset that has prevailed for decades. This revolution cannot occur overnight. It demands time, deliberate effort, and unwavering dedication. As I continued to reshape my beliefs, nurturing healthier perspectives and bolstering self-awareness, my attitude underwent a profound transformation despite numerous failures and challenges. This process is ongoing in me; it requires a lifelong commitment to making a difference within oneself. Changing one's mindset is not confined to a singular moment—it permeates every aspect of existence, every single day.

Recognizing the journey, rather than the destination, as the focal point of life allows disruptive leaders to immerse themselves fully in the present moment. They can appreciate the small victories, cease to worry about little obstacles, and forge meaningful connections that contribute to their personal and professional growth.

Now is the perfect time to embark on your personal journey of mindset transformation.

Dare to dream big. Challenge your beliefs. Embrace new opportunities. Cultivate an unwavering determination to make a lasting impact. Create robust relationships and networks that drive change.

The power of a shifted mindset knows no boundaries and has the potential to change not only your life but also the lives of those around you. Let this journey be the catalyst that propels you forward onto a path of perpetual growth and extraordinary possibilities.

CHAPTER 3
Find a Disruptive Higher Purpose

The secret of success is the constancy of purpose.
—*Benjamin Disraeli*[18]

A Profound Realization

I was skeptical about most vision-and-mission statements for decades. Many seemed like nothing more than fabricated marketing tools and public relations exercises. They lacked genuine reflection of an organization's mission, values, and goals. I've been proven right by numerous high-profile organizations that have demonstrated these statements were empty words, not backed with meaningful actions. Nor did they (the leadership) hold themselves accountable for tangible results beyond stock price and profits. It didn't help that they changed or updated their purpose statements annually, along with their business plan. Instead of giving people confidence in the organization, they've shown an inconsistency in their actions and a lack of long-term commitment. It left me questioning the authenticity and credibility of these statements.

Then COVID hit. Its impact was nothing like we'd seen in our lifetimes, turning lives upside down and leaving humanity collectively pondering the *why* behind our actions. We saw, suddenly, a need for a meaningful existence in the face of a crisis. As uncertainty loomed, the importance of true purpose became undeniable.

---

[18] Benjamin Disraeli, in a speech to the National Union of Conservative and Constitutional Associations, London, 24 June 1872, quoted in *Selected Speeches of the Late Right Honourable the Earl of Beaconsfield, Volume II*, edited by T. E. Kebbel, 1882.

It was during this time that I had a profound realization. I understood that most of my previous successes were connected to a higher purpose, even if that connection was not always consciously apparent. Looking back, I discovered the underlying reasons why I had left jobs despite holding senior positions and doing well financially. I always felt a longing to find and embrace a higher purpose, something that would give my work and life meaning and fulfillment. During my life's journey, I discovered that building and evolving a higher purpose was both challenging and deeply rewarding as it became the foundation of our motivation and daily actions.

I reflected on my involvement in starting new businesses, both as an entrepreneur and in global professional services firms. I found that unless there was a clear and disruptive higher purpose, I couldn't motivate myself to embark on the journey. It became clear that a purpose beyond profits, capable of making a positive impact on the world, is what truly ignited my passion and drove me forward.

Although skepticism clouded my perception of vision and mission statements for years, the COVID experience altered that perception. I had a profound realization that a clear, higher purpose at both individual and organizational levels, when fully aligned, drives transformative change and positive impact that benefits thousands, sometimes millions, of people.

I suggest five reasons for finding your higher purpose in life and how it relates to professional and personal success:

Meaningful Direction

COVID-19 caused widespread confusion and mixed responses worldwide. People fell in line behind leaders who focused on the interests of the entire community, communicated a clear way forward, and highlighted the need for a sense of direction and meaning. I witnessed how that higher purpose acted as a beacon of inspiration that offered individuals and companies a clear sense of a mission, values, and goals.

It became a guiding light that helped navigate difficult times and guided decision-making. At the start of the lockdowns (in March 2020), when the pandemic forced us to work from home, a wave of confusion, disorientation, and even hopelessness swept over many people. There were no immediate solutions to help us face this uncommon challenge.

In the face of adversity, I made a resolute decision to hold daily meetings with some of my key leaders and weekly gatherings with the entire team. These served as powerful reminders of our collective mission, the driving force behind the journey to build GHD Digital. We developed new thought leadership and intensified our engagement with communities on social media platforms during this challenging period. Social media allowed me to connect with a diverse range of people who shared our dedication to a higher purpose. So we embarked on an endeavor to accelerate community engagement. With consistent reflection on our higher purpose, we maintained the unity of our team and also ignited a renewed sense of vigor among the personal and professional challenges that surrounded us.

Employee Engagement

The pandemic reshaped the traditional work environment with remote setups and increased stress. In our business, we could see that our higher purpose fostered increased employee engagement because it connected them to something greater than the daily grind. It gave them a sense of fulfillment, drove motivation, and encouraged a sense of belonging within the wider GHD organization. While many of our competitors resorted to cutting staff during the pandemic, we committed to upholding our core values. We took a firm stand from the first week of lockdowns and remote work. There would be no widespread layoffs or salary cuts during this time of uncertainty. If there was not much work, we distributed it equitably among all employees. The only exemption to this arrangement was the most senior managers and executives, who voluntarily opted to reduce their working hours.

This was a brilliant move and a highly-visionary approach which the whole executive team endorsed less than hours after the lockdowns were imposed. It was an immensely proud moment to witness such exemplary leadership from the top, and it generated an astonishing impact on the unwavering support and engagement of employees. This decisive action by GHD leaders will forever be etched in the memories of many as a remarkable demonstration of truly living our values when they mattered most.

Adaptability and Resilience

A higher purpose instills a resilient mindset by emphasizing the need to overcome challenges and adapt to changing circumstances. It helps individuals and companies bounce back, reinvent themselves, and create innovative solutions to address new problems.

The world faced immense risks during this time and remote work became the norm in many countries. But something weighed heavily on my heart. I worried that our people would struggle with the absence of human connection precisely at a time when our clients sought help and guidance.

I encouraged my leaders to exemplify the power of digital technology and innovative thinking instead of retreating into isolation. Our mission was clear: we aimed to double interactions with clients to ensure that our insights were not only relevant but also deeply connected to the challenges they faced—be it working from home, shutting down operations, or persisting amid uncertainty.

And so we embarked upon an extraordinary journey. Our thought leadership and online forum output surged dramatically. We engaged our people and lifted their spirits above the prevailing pandemic fears. We extended our networks, finding ways to connect face-to-face with executives who were typically elusive due to their demanding travel schedules but were now more accessible.

This unwavering dedication nurtured a workforce that was adaptable and resilient. We also forged deep relationships with our clients, partners, and communities. We rose above the challenges and demonstrated the boundless potential of human resolve and the enduring strength of unity.

Building Motivation through Trust and Loyalty

Our higher purpose demonstrated a genuine commitment to societal and environmental issues. We saw that customers, employees, and shareholders were more inclined to stay loyal to companies that actively strove to make a positive impact beyond profit.

A disruptive higher purpose has the capacity to fuel motivation through the trust and loyalty of people in a significant manner. When they engage with a purpose larger than themselves, it deeply resonates with their core values and beliefs, imparting a profound sense of significance and satisfaction in their endeavors. This harmony cultivates a foundation of trust between individuals and the organization or causes they are dedicated to.

For example, a team of doctors, who are my friends, works tirelessly in a free clinic to provide essential medical services to underserved communities in India, Bangladesh, and Nepal. Their commitment and passion for addressing healthcare disparities reflect a shared purpose that goes beyond individual interests, instilling a sense of fulfillment and unity in their work.

As individuals embrace and uphold a disruptive higher purpose, they willingly invest their time, energy, and expertise with unwavering dedication. This commitment originates from a sincere conviction in the transformative influence of their actions toward advancing the collective purpose. Consequently, a culture of trust is nurtured, fostering an environment where individuals feel appreciated and esteemed for their contributions toward a common objective.

Based on my experience, when individuals are deeply connected to a disruptive higher purpose like the one we had for GHD Digital, loyalty naturally blossoms. People are more inclined to persist through obstacles and setbacks, recognizing that their endeavors contribute to something valuable and impactful. This allegiance fosters a spirit of solidarity and cohesion among team members, establishing a supportive ecosystem where collaboration flourishes.

In summary, a disruptive higher purpose acts as a guiding light that motivates and inspires individuals to excel, nurturing trust and loyalty among them. By aligning personal values with a shared mission, people feel empowered and impassioned to achieve extraordinary outcomes, paving the way for a culture characterized by mutual respect, encouragement, and unwavering commitment.

Attracting and Retaining Talent

The expectations of job seekers changed during the pandemic. Potential employees increasingly prioritized meaningful work that aligned with their values and contributed to a greater purpose. Companies that could articulate a higher purpose were more likely to attract and retain top talent, as people were seeking to make a difference in the world and be part of organizations that shared their same vision.

In the early months of 2020, GHD Digital was a young business facing the challenge of attracting top talent due to the misconception that we were solely an engineering firm with limited expertise in the digital realm. Recognizing this, we set out to redefine our brand and establish ourselves as leaders in the digital landscape.

To accomplish this, we honed our focus on addressing real-world issues that truly mattered, such as climate change, sustainability, and the future of communities. Our dedication to making a difference in these areas acted as a powerful magnet. We attracted exceptional individuals driven by the desire to contribute to solving the world's greatest challenges.

When the pandemic took a tighter grip on the world, it became even more apparent that embracing a higher purpose was not a choice but a necessity. It served as a driving force for both individuals and companies, provided meaning, and fueled employee engagement. With a higher purpose guiding our actions, we could adapt and remain resilient in the face of uncertainty.

We demonstrated our commitment to creating a better future by aligning ourselves with causes that truly matter. This, in turn, attracted even more talented individuals to join our cause, as they were inspired by the opportunity to work in a company that actively sought to make a positive impact.

In fact, the pandemic served to reinforce what we should've already known: a higher purpose has tremendous value in inspiring individuals and companies. It injected a sense of meaning into our work, enhanced employee engagement, fostered adaptability and resilience, built trust, and attracted exceptional talent. Embracing a higher purpose with an innovative mindset allowed us to confidently navigate an uncertain landscape and contribute to shaping a brighter future for all.

Disruptive Higher Purpose

A disruptive higher purpose is a vision that challenges the status quo and creates an existential reason for significant change or innovation in a particular industry or field to benefit others. It goes beyond traditional business objectives and metrics and aims to create a meaningful impact by addressing industry, societal, or environmental issues. Being disruptive challenges existing methods and people and requires an upfront investment to achieve a longer-term payoff. Of course, this is far from easy. Organizations must also sustain a healthy financial position and support from shareholders, investors, and other key stakeholders while seeking this higher purpose. Many organizations do not sustain the trade-offs. Stock markets can be brutal when the financial results of those embracing a disruptive higher purpose are not as promised.

In 2017, GHD acquired my company, Technova, and I joined its leadership team. This was an opportunity to shape my life's purpose and do something meaningful. We established GHD Digital in 2018 to provide a disruptive higher purpose. We chose to help transform not only our near-century-old company but also the entire $200 billion AEC industry. It enabled us to develop a vision owned by the leadership team that challenged the industry's status quo and relatively low levels of digital maturity and provided innovative opportunities for the whole industry.

Five years later, renowned Harvard Business School professor Ranjay Gulati unveiled his latest literary masterpiece, *Deep Purpose*, which has valuable insights from more than two hundred executive interviews across eighteen companies. This thought-provoking book presents a compelling argument for revolutionary approaches in business and the extraordinary outcomes they can yield to benefit both companies and society.

Professor Gulati passionately asserts that deep purpose must be ingrained into the very essence of organizations, transcending the superficial and serving as an innovative framework for optimal functionality. Embracing profound purpose acts as a catalyst, igniting a paradigm shift in business operations that will result in remarkable advantages for all stakeholders. Within these inspired lines lies a revelation that could reshape the future of business as we know it.

> *Most leaders think of purpose functionally or instrumentally, regarding it as a tool they can wield. Deep purpose leaders think of it as something more fundamental: an existential statement that expresses the firm's very reason for being. Rather than simply pursuing a purpose, these leaders project it faithfully out onto the world. In their hands, purpose serves as an organizing principle that shapes decision-making and binds stakeholders to one another.*
>
> *—Ranjay Gulati*[19]

Unlike a regular, run-of-the-mill mission statement, a disruptive higher purpose statement seeks to challenge established norms, often questioning existing systems and practices. It inspires individuals or organizations to think differently and take bold actions to drive change. A disruptive higher purpose reimagines traditional approaches and pushes boundaries to create innovative solutions. It encourages businesses and individuals to align their efforts and take action to accomplish larger societal or environmental goals. By leveraging disruptive technologies, novel business models, or unconventional practices, it strives to create a positive impact on a larger scale.

Examples of companies with disruptive higher purpose include companies using electric vehicles to revolutionize transportation or education through online platforms. Other examples include the following:

- **TOMS** is a footwear company that is making a significant impact with its "One for One" business model. For every pair of shoes bought; a pair is donated to a child in need. This is a socially driven approach designed to improve the lives of others, and it resonates with consumers worldwide. TOMS extended its impact beyond shoes and now supports initiatives such as eye care, safe water access, and maternal health. Its disruptive higher purpose benefits those in need and contributes to brand growth and customer loyalty.

---

[19] Ranjay Gulati, *Deep Purpose: The Heart and Soul of High-Performance Companies*. New York City: Harper Business, an imprint of Harper-Collins, 2022.

- **Danone** is a multinational food product corporation that stands out for its social and environmental goals. The company has a strong commitment to promoting health and well-being through its products. Danone's "One Planet, One Health" vision encapsulates its higher purpose of creating sustainable value for stakeholders across the globe. This includes reducing greenhouse gases, promoting regenerative agriculture, and empowering local communities. By aligning its purpose with social goals, Danone has built trust among consumers and investors while making a positive impact on the planet.
- **Warby Parker** is an eyewear company that integrates social wellbeing into its business model through the "Buy a Pair, Give a Pair" program. For every pair of glasses sold, it donates a pair to someone in need. This approach aligns with the company's higher purpose of improving vision health among underserved communities.

Ultimately, a disruptive higher purpose seeks to redefine the possibilities to make a lasting, positive impact on society and the world.

What Compromises Disruptive Higher Purpose?

Disruptive leaders do the right thing for their stakeholders. Prioritizing short-term profits or key performance indicators (KPIs) without progressing toward a longer-term purpose can eventually destroy a company in multiple ways. Some companies focus solely on maximizing short-term outcomes to deliver bonuses to executives and dividends to shareholders. Such businesses create an environment where compromising ethical standards and engaging in questionable practices is acceptable. These can include cutting corners, disregarding compliance regulations, or exploiting employees and suppliers to reduce costs. Sometimes, management is just "mining the quarry"—not worrying about the cost of rectification or the limited life of the business.

At other times, short-term measures are directly driving financial rewards to leaders who do what is needed to gain high returns and then jump out before the failure of the strategy is obvious. Such actions can damage the company's reputation, erode trust among stakeholders, and result in legal consequences, including costly lawsuits. Various factors can compromise a higher purpose within an organization, including these:

- **Prioritizing the Short-term**. Seeking profit or KPIs without a balanced consideration of long-term implications can compromise integrity and long-term viability. This may involve making decisions solely based on financial considerations and neglecting the impact on stakeholders or the broader mission.
- **Lack of Alignment**. A higher purpose not aligned with a company's core values and mission undermines the credibility and authenticity of its purpose.
- **Inconsistent Actions**. When a company's actions and practices do not align with its higher purpose, employees and stakeholders question its authenticity, which erodes trust and credibility.
- **Inconsistent Messaging**. Failing to effectively communicate the higher purpose to employees, customers, and stakeholders damages effectiveness. Clear, consistent communication is essential.
- **Internal Conflicts**. Internal conflicts, power struggles, or siloed departments make it challenging to align actions and decisions with the higher purpose and hinder its implementation.
- **Lack of Employee Empowerment**. Employees lacking the autonomy and authority to contribute meaningfully to the higher purpose become disengaged and frustrated. Empowering employees is crucial to sustaining their motivation and commitment.
- **Unethical Practices**. Compromising values in pursuit of a higher purpose damages the company's reputation and undermines trust. Ethical practices must align with the purpose in order to maintain organizational integrity.

- **Lack of Accountability**. Failure to hold individuals or departments accountable for actions that contradict the higher purpose often leads to unethical behavior.
- **Lack of Evaluation and Adaptation**. A higher-purpose statement shouldn't change with the annual business plan. However, regular evaluation and honing of the higher purpose are necessary to address evolving societal needs and prevent its irrelevance over time.
- **External Pressures**. Succumbing to market trends, competitive forces, or shareholder demands can compromise the higher purpose if they take precedence over the core mission.
- **Lack of Investment**. A narrow focus can lead to a lack of investment in research and development, employee training, or infrastructure improvement. Competitors who prioritize purpose-driven strategies usually outperform companies dominated by short-term goals, leaving them unable to effectively compete in the market.

Ultimately, without a clear purpose beyond short-term gains, companies risk losing the support of customers, employees, and investors, which can lead to the very problems they were created to solve. Some recent examples include these:

- **Wells Fargo** was involved in a 2016 scandal where employees opened millions of unauthorized accounts to meet aggressive sales targets. The company faced significant backlash and was fined billions of dollars for its unethical practices.
- **Uber** faced numerous controversies related to ethical concerns, including allegations of sexual harassment within the company, aggressive tactics against rivals and regulators, and the use of software to evade law enforcement. These practices tarnished the company's image and resulted in the resignation of its CEO.
- **Theranos** was a healthcare technology company that claimed to have developed revolutionary blood testing technology. It was later exposed as a fraud—the company misled investors and regulators about the effectiveness of its technology. This compromised the

company's purpose of revolutionizing healthcare for short-term financial gains and led to serious jail time for the CEO, who oversaw it all.

These incidents highlight how solely prioritizing profit without a clear purpose—including a commitment to ethical behavior—devastates companies. Sadly, there are hundreds of other examples of corporate failure. It's like the world does not learn this lesson. Companies should strive for a purpose beyond financial gain by focusing on creating value for all stakeholders while maintaining ethical standards.

It's also essential for an organization's culture to foster and support its higher purpose. A misaligned culture can undermine influence and sustainability. The values and principles underlying the organization's purpose should be embedded in the corporate culture. It should become a subconscious, automatic action, a framework through which all stakeholders view their world. Addressing these factors and maintaining a strong commitment to the higher purpose is imperative to ensure its integrity and effectiveness.

Disruptive Higher Purpose Creates Synergy and Builds Resilience

You may get to the very top of the ladder,
and then find it has not been leaning against the right wall.

—Allen Raine[20]

A disruptive higher purpose can be a guiding force that helps leaders navigate challenging times. It provides them

---

[20] Attributed to many sources, the earliest known version of this idea is attributed to Allen Raine, possibly a pseudonym for Welsh novelist Anne Adaliza Evans Puddicombe. First printed in *The Brooklyn Daily Eagle*. Brooklyn, NY: Frank D. Shroth. Read the complete investigation at https://quoteinvestigator.com/2017/08/17/ladder/#f+16683+1+1, accessed 21 February 2024.

with a sense of meaning and direction. During my journey of starting businesses, I frequently faced adversity. Having a clear understanding of my higher purpose instilled a sense of resilience and determination that helped me overcome obstacles.

During challenging times, it's easy to feel overwhelmed, lose motivation, or have a negative mindset, which encourages shortcuts and short-term thinking. However, a clear, disruptive, higher purpose reignites the energy within me and reminds me of the impact I am trying to make. It serves as a constant "beacon of hope" of why I do what I do and gives me the strength to persevere and do what is important instead of what is easy. It allows startup founders and entrepreneurs to view setbacks and failures as opportunities for growth and learning. Instead of feeling discouraged, we are fueled by the belief that challenges are steppingstones rather than stumbling blocks. This mindset helps us bounce back from setbacks, find new ways, and adapt our strategies to move forward.

A disruptive higher purpose taps into your passion, values, and beliefs to connect them to something greater than yourself. This provides a sense of fulfillment, even during difficult moments. It shifts the focus from immediate struggles to the long-term vision so you can maintain perspective and stay committed to your goals. It fosters a sense of connection with others who share similar goals. It creates a community of like-minded individuals who can support and inspire each other through challenging times. Collaborating with others aligned with a higher purpose enhances creativity, problem-solving, and overall motivation.

Disruptive Higher Purpose Links Business to Social Good

The link between social good and a higher purpose is deeply intertwined. Higher purpose refers to an individual's sense of meaning, goals, and values that extend beyond personal gain. It often involves contributing to the well-being of others and making a positive impact on the world.

Social good, on the other hand, is the pursuit of actions, initiatives, or projects that promote the welfare and betterment of the whole society. It encompasses areas such as environmental sustainability, social justice, equality, education, healthcare, and more. It speaks to needs that are beyond just paychecks for employees and profits for shareholders.

When higher purpose and social good align, it creates a ripple effect. As individuals pursue social good, they inspire and motivate others to do the same and cultivate a collective effort toward creating a more equitable, compassionate, and sustainable world. This synergy amplifies the impact and effectiveness of social-good initiatives and fosters a sense of connection and unity among those committed to a higher purpose and social good.

Years ago, pollution was a far greater problem in the US than it is today. Companies dumped waste on the ground, allowing toxic chemicals to seep into groundwater or pumped waste into rivers. These pollutants became serious health risks for residents in places like the Love Canal neighborhood in Niagara Falls, New York. Responding to the failure of businesses to adopt a higher purpose, a powerful environmental consciousness movement emerged. In 1980, the US Congress became a disruptive leader. It created regulatory frameworks to address environmental carnage and created governance structures within the Environmental Protection Agency with a funding and accountability model via "Superfunds." It was allocated the responsibility, along with the organizations that contributed to the pollution, to clean up these sites. Waste disposal regulations were tightened, and many dangerous situations were made safe, though remediation continues more than four decades later.

Environmentalism was one of the most disruptive leadership advances of the late twentieth century. The recognition of the limitations of the earth's resources and the need for increasingly careful stewardship over those resources changed the way Americans did business. Today's zero-carbon footprint goals are direct descendants of those early social purpose crusades.

The leadership to achieve the changes required for net-zero by 2050 can only be delivered with disruptive leadership.

Despite many gains, companies need to consider social purpose more than they do. If you look at the American way of doing business, people in many organizations do not see it as a driving factor. Advances in nutrition, physical conditioning, and healthcare means people live longer. According to United Nations estimates, the earth's population reached 8 billion in November 2022.[21] The largest portion of that growth is occurring in some of the poorest countries on the planet.

How can we utilize technology to address water, energy, and food scarcity? How should your organization look at water or food insecurity in different parts of the world? What does your company do that could alleviate these and other challenges, like the lack of education, rampant diseases, crime, human trafficking, and so on?

The social-good portion of a higher purpose statement can and should encompass the underprivileged. These can be in your local community. They invariably are if you live in a large city, but smaller towns are not immune. They are also elsewhere in your country and around the world. America is one of the wealthiest nations on earth, and some of the most successful companies could use a disruptive higher purpose to help alleviate the challenges of humanity.

Social good is not charity or optional when we talk about a disruptive higher purpose. It's an integral part of what makes the higher purpose disruptive and meaningful. It's said that businesses are better than governments at getting things done because businesses must earn profits to stay in business. Look at the US "war on poverty" and "war on drugs"—initiatives from the 1970s. Half a century later, after spending trillions of dollars on each, poverty and drugs remain major societal

---

[21] "Day of Eight Billion," UN.org. New York: United Nations, (undated). https://www.un.org/en/dayof8billion#:~:text=Day%20of%20Eight%20 Billion,a%20milestone%20in%20human%20development, accessed 22 Aug 2023.

problems. Governments simply do not have the resources or commitment they need, and this is where companies and individuals with a disruptive higher purpose can help address these challenges. Some positive examples are the following:

- **Ben & Jerry's** is an ice cream company that has long advocated corporate social responsibility. It incorporates its higher purpose of social justice and environmental sustainability into its business practices. Ben & Jerry's sources fair trade ingredients, supports social causes and strives for environmental sustainability.
- **Seventh Generation** is a household and personal-care products company that prioritizes sustainability and environmental responsibility. Its products are eco-friendly, non-toxic, and responsibly-sourced. The company actively campaigns for policies that promote environmental protection and inspire consumer awareness.
- **The Body Shop** is a cosmetics and skincare company with a strong focus on cruelty-free products, fair-trade ingredients, and community-trade initiatives. The brand's higher purpose revolves around creating positive social change through responsible business practices.

The link between social good and disruptive higher purpose lies in the shared intention of making a positive impact on society while conducting a profitable business. Aligning one's higher purpose with social good not only provides a sense of meaning and direction but also fuels resilience, energizes individuals, and fosters a collective effort toward creating a better world.

Disruptive Higher Purpose Helps Us Think Big

A disruptive higher purpose has the power to inspire people to think big and make bold moves. When someone embraces a higher purpose that challenges the status quo and disrupts conventional thinking, it propels them to push beyond their comfort zones. Having a disruptive higher purpose encourages individuals to break free from conventional limitations or preconceived ideas of what is possible. It ignites a deep passion and determination to create a meaningful purpose and make a lasting impact. People driven by a disruptive higher purpose willingly take more risks, challenge existing norms, and pursue innovative approaches.

It also attracts like-minded individuals who share the same desire for innovation and creates a collective energy and momentum that brings together a community of individuals motivated and aligned by the same purpose. This collaborative effort amplifies the potential for big ideas and big moves as diverse talents and perspectives converge to tackle the challenges.

Conventional wisdom, like "Slow and steady wins the race" or "Rome wasn't built in a day," advises us to take small, incremental steps to achieve success. Why, then, make large, bold moves?

Let me be clear: If you want to build a house, then you nail one board at a time. If you want to run a marathon, then you must first learn to run a mile. Slow and steady, in its place, is always valuable and sometimes necessary. But building a house or running a marathon will not change the world—your life, possibly, but not the world.

Large, bold moves change the status quo. If you want to change the world and transform the lives of thousands of people, you first need their attention. You need to engage them to keep their attention, and technology has made that a lot easier. Without some of the latest twentieth and twenty-first-century innovations, like social media and online shopping, life would be very different. Platforms like LinkedIn, Facebook, Amazon, or eBay are the outcomes of bold visions by entrepreneurs who started them by saying, "Why not?" and built from there. These platforms and others continue to have a transformational impact on our lives. Their creators now rank among the most influential people of all time.

The combination of a bold vision with a common higher purpose among believers gives you the best opportunity to serve the communities that you care about.

A disruptive higher purpose fuels a mindset of thinking big and making big moves by challenging existing paradigms, pushing boundaries, attracting like-minded individuals, and fostering a collective drive to create significant positive change.

Disruptive Higher Purpose and Profit

The dilemma between higher purpose and profit within companies arises from the tension between pursuing financial success and fulfilling a broader societal mission.

Profit is necessary. It enables businesses to grow, invest in innovation, and provide returns to stakeholders. The pursuit of profit involves optimizing business practices, increasing efficiency, and generating revenue to benefit the company's bottom line.

Meanwhile, a disruptive higher purpose commits a company to making a positive impact beyond financial gains. This purpose could be centered around addressing social, environmental, or ethical issues and aligning the company's activities with the greater good. Such companies prioritize creating shared value for all stakeholders, including employees, customers, communities, and the environment.

A dilemma arises when companies struggle to balance maximizing profit and fulfilling their higher purpose. Increasing profitability may sometimes require compromising on social or environmental responsibilities. For example, a company may be tempted to cut corners or exploit resources to increase profits, even if it contradicts its stated purpose.

Organizations face a critical decision when short-term profitability and long-term purposes seem irreconcilable. Prioritizing short-term profitability may bring immediate financial gains but can jeopardize the long-term vision and impact what an organization seeks to achieve through its higher purpose.

To navigate this dilemma, companies must adopt strategies that align profit-making with its higher purpose. This could involve innovating to diversify, integrating sustainability practices, promoting diversity and inclusion, supporting local communities, or investing in fast-tracking net-zero carbon release. Incorporating these values into core business functions and decision-making processes creates a win-win situation that benefits the organization's financial performance and positive impact.

Balancing short-term profitability with long-term higher purpose requires strategic thinking and effective decision-making. A company needs to take steps to align its actions and higher purpose by integrating them into the organization's core values, mission statements, and operational strategies. This involves adopting a more holistic, forward-thinking approach and seeking win-win outcomes where short-term profitability aligns with long-term higher-purpose outcomes. It's possible to pursue sustainable business practices, engage in ethical behaviors, invest in innovation and research, build strong relationships with stakeholders, and consistently communicate a commitment toward a higher purpose. Emphasizing the interconnectedness of short-term and long-term goals can lead to both financial success and positive societal impact.

Leaders play a crucial role in navigating the short-term earnings versus the higher-purpose conflict. They must articulate and communicate the higher purpose effectively to ensure that it resonates with employees, customers, and investors. By seeking alignment between earnings and purpose, leaders can foster a culture that values both financial success and meaningful impact.

Ultimately, balancing earnings and higher purpose requires a shift in mindset and a new commitment to value-driven decision-making. By integrating purpose, business strategies, and operations, organizations can create a sustainable and impactful business model that delivers financial success and social good.

Profit and purpose are not mutually exclusive—they are two sides of the same coin.

Disruptive Higher Purpose Enables Trust

When a company establishes a disruptive higher purpose that aims to address significant societal or environmental issues, it can inspire trust in several ways:

- **Accountability and Impact Measurement**. A disruptive higher purpose comes with a commitment to measuring and reporting social and environmental impacts. By holding themselves accountable for their actions and regularly sharing progress and results, companies earn greater trust from stakeholders who value accountability.
- **Alignment with Values**. A disruptive higher purpose aligns with the values and beliefs of employees and customers. When individuals see a company actively working toward a cause they care about, it creates a sense of shared values and builds trust.
- **Authenticity and Transparency**. A company that genuinely embraces a disruptive higher purpose tends to be more transparent and authentic in its actions. This builds trust as stakeholders perceive the company as being open and honest about its intentions and practices.
- **Employee Engagement and Motivation**. A company truly demonstrating a disruptive higher purpose significantly impacts employee engagement. When employees know that their work contributes to a purpose beyond just making money, they become more motivated, loyal, and committed. This increased engagement fosters trust between employees and the company.
- **Long-term Perspective**. A disruptive higher purpose requires a long-term commitment to a cause or

mission. Companies demonstrate their dedication to creating sustainable and meaningful change by emphasizing a vision that extends beyond short-term profits. This long-term perspective builds trust among stakeholders who see the company as more than just a profit-driven entity.

Overall, a disruptive higher purpose can help build trust by aligning with values, demonstrating authenticity, embracing a long-term perspective, promoting accountability, and driving employee engagement. These elements create a sense of trustworthiness that resonates with stakeholders and positions the company as one that prioritizes innovation alongside financial success.

Exceptional Talent Needs a Disruptive Higher Purpose

The purpose of life is not to be happy. It is to be useful, to be honorable, to be compassionate, to have it make some difference that you have lived and lived well. It's, above all, to matter: to count, to stand for something, to have made some difference that you lived at all.

–Leo Rosten[22]

In today's dynamic workforce, employees no longer solely seek traditional, nine-to-five jobs. They want more than just a regular paycheck. Instead, people are looking for opportunities that align with their passion, offer flexibility and work-life balance, foster personal and professional growth, and provide a sense of purpose and fulfillment. They want to be part of organizations that value their unique skills, acknowledge their contributions, and create a positive, inclusive work environment.

---

[22] Attributed, probably compiled from several similar statements by Rosten. Read the entire investigation at: https://quoteinvestigator.com/2014/11/29/purpose/, accessed 27 February 2024.

To attract and retain top talent, companies must recognize that employees seek a holistic experience beyond the conventional notion of work. A disruptive higher purpose can play a significant role in attracting and retaining talent within a company. When an organization is guided by such a purpose, it appeals to individuals who seek more than just a traditional job.

Outdoor clothing and gear company Patagonia, for example, has a strong reputation for its commitment to environmental sustainability and social responsibility. Its mission "to save our home planet" includes initiatives like regenerative organic farming, reducing waste through product lifecycle efforts, and advocating for public land conservation.

Because of its clear, higher purpose, Patagonia successfully attracts talented individuals who are also passionate about making a positive environmental impact. Many employees are not only motivated by the quality of the products but also by the company's commitment to creating a sustainable future. They view their work as more than just a job. They view it as an opportunity to contribute to something greater than themselves alone. Patagonia now ranks as a stellar example of using higher purpose as a powerful tool in attracting and retaining top talent.

Following are ten ways a higher purpose can help talent attraction and retention:

1. **Meaningful Work**. It gives employees a sense of fulfillment and meaning in their work, making them more likely to stay with the company.
2. **Alignment of Values**. It attracts individuals who share similar values and beliefs, leading to a stronger alignment between employee motivations and organizational goals.
3. **Sense of Impact**. When employees see their work having a positive impact on society or the environment, they become committed to supporting the company.
4. **Personal Growth and Development**. It often pushes companies to invest in employee development, which

enhances skill sets and provides growth opportunities that attract and retain talented individuals.
5. **Stronger Employee Engagement**. It ignites passion and engagement among employees, fosters a positive work culture, and increases employee satisfaction and loyalty.
6. **Attracting Like-minded Talent**. A clear higher purpose helps a company attract individuals who are passionate about the same cause, which creates a community of like-minded colleagues and fosters a supportive work environment.
7. **Differentiation from Competitors**. Having a disruptive higher purpose differentiates a company from its competitors, making it more attractive to top talent who seek organizations with a unique and impactful vision.
8. **Employee Empowerment**. It provides employees with a sense of empowerment because they are contributing to a greater purpose than their individual roles. This empowers them to take ownership and responsibility and enhances retention.
9. **Enhanced Company Reputation**. A company known for its higher purpose gains a positive reputation in the market and makes it an employer of choice for talented individuals who want to be associated with such organizations.
10. **Long-term Sustainability**. It's often associated with a long-term vision, which creates stability and security for employees and attracts and retains those who seek a stable and purpose-driven career path.

These are just some reasons why a higher purpose can help attract and retain talent. It creates an environment that fosters personal growth, engagement, and a sense of impact and appeals to individuals who feel aligned with the company's values and vision.

Finding a disruptive higher purpose gives you meaningful direction that does not solely focus on profit but links business to social good. It creates synergy, builds resilience, and helps you to think big. A higher purpose earns trust from others when your values align and you demonstrate authenticity.

CHAPTER 4

Disrupt Your Comfort Zone and Inertia

Pushing the boundaries of our comfort zones gives us immense power to mold our beliefs and choices and, ultimately, shape the course of our lives. It's a truth that is often unnoticed or underappreciated.

I hold people who can push their boundaries in high esteem. They radiate an unwavering spirit and display exceptional strength, take risks, and master the art of resilience. Remarkable leaders actively seek challenges and extend their limits in a relentless pursuit of their passions that surpass self-interest for the benefit of others. They refuse to settle for a life of mediocrity. Instead, they choose to embrace adversity, persisting with unwavering determination even in the face of seemingly insurmountable obstacles that sometimes come from their peers and superiors. An unwavering commitment to serve others and refusal to allow setbacks to hold them back is a testament to the incredible power we all have within. Remarkable leaders live their lives outside their comfort zone, motivated by their passion for their higher purpose. I can relate to how they feel and why they behave the way they do, as it's what I aspire to in my life.

The Comfort Zone and Why People Love It

The modern comforts and conveniences that now most influence our daily experience—cars, computers, television, climate control, smartphones, ultra-processed food, and more—have been used by our species for about 100 years or less. That's around 0.03 percent of the time we've walked the earth. Include all the Homos—habilis, erectus, heidelbergensis, neanderthalensis, and us—and open the time scale to 2.5 million years and the figure drops to 0.004 percent. Constant comfort is a radically new thing for us humans.

—Michael Easter[23]

This book is intended to be a resource designed for leaders who aspire to embrace courage, transcend boundaries, and revolutionize the status quo. It's important, however, that our approach does not divide individuals into "good versus bad" categories as we strive to engage all readers. Rather, we aim to distinguish between exceptional followers and exceptional leaders. While some may find comfort in the present circumstances, they possess the ability to rally behind far-seeing leaders who dare to envision a future filled with boundless possibilities.

When a person is in their "comfort zone," they feel safe, secure, and satisfied with life. They are happy with the way things are and expect things to continue in the same direction. Sometimes, they have a fear of the unknown. The apprehension toward the unknown is a dynamic interplay, as it stems not only from individual caution but also from the organizational structures that discourage risk-taking. When mistakes are met with retribution, they foster a culture that vehemently clings to the comfort zone, further perpetuating the fear of embracing change.

A person's comfort zone is also characterized by a lack of desire for a challenge, a lack of motivation to do things differently, and a risk-averse attitude. Stepping outside this zone means dealing with uncertainty, facing new challenges, and potentially encountering failure.

Change does not happen automatically in your comfort zone. It occurs when you step beyond familiar boundaries. We know from life experience this is true in different areas of life—

---

[23] Michael Easter, *The Comfort Crisis: Embrace Discomfort to Reclaim Your Wild, Happy, Healthy Self*. New York City: Rodale Books (an imprint of Penguin Random House), 2021.

physically, mentally, spiritually, and financially. Your comfort zone is limiting, so you may remain stagnant because you feel change is impossible. Only by venturing beyond these limits can you achieve progress and growth. An example of this is physical fitness. When you push your body past comfortable exercise, you challenge your muscles so they strengthen and build endurance. Similarly, by stepping outside your comfort zone, you embark on a journey toward profound personal development.

Nevertheless, breaking free of self-imposed boundaries does not require a drastic departure from the norm. But it's important to recognize stretching too much or going too far all at once can trigger distress that is counterproductive. Therefore, balancing how far we go is also important. Starting out by taking small steps beyond our boundaries can trigger significant growth. Consistently engaging in this practice, day after day, week after week, and month after month, gradually expands our limits and leads to substantial personal expansion.

To achieve disruptive results, we must boldly push our limits. Growth and development flourish when we operate at the very edge of what feels safe and familiar. It may be tempting to shy away from discomfort, but the world we live in demands that we disrupt what makes us feel safe.

Excellence is about stepping outside the comfort zone, training with a spirit of endeavor, and accepting the inevitability of trials and tribulations. Progress is built, in effect, upon the foundations of necessary failure. That is the essential paradox of expert performance.

−Matthew Syed[24]

Proposing changes can trigger people to move instantly into their "discomfort zone." They resist change, new ideas,

[24] Matthew Syed, *Bounce: Mozart, Federer, Picasso, Beckham, and the Science of Success.* New York City: HarperCollins, 2011.

or protocols and may resist taking on new responsibilities. Many people you encounter daily live in their comfort zone with no intention of changing. There is a lack of growth of missed opportunities, and it creates an environment where organizations cannot progress or grow as well as they should.

Some people prefer to live with a sense of familiarity and security. Stepping beyond this means confronting uncertainty, embracing new challenges, and dealing with possible failure. It takes courage and determination. We need to take risks and push ourselves to grow and adapt. Embracing discomfort is the path to personal and professional development, expanded skill sets, and new opportunities. The initial discomfort is a small price to pay for the rewards that await.

Personal courage, however, cannot be the sole determining factor. It's worth noting that many individuals who appear conservative in a professional setting may willingly engage in daring activities such as skydiving or bungee jumping. Their hesitation lies not in inherent risk aversion but rather in a workplace environment that fails to reward risk-taking.

The predominant obstacle to disruptive leadership in businesses, in my view, lies in corporate culture. This culture not only discourages risk but also stigmatizes acts of courage. It's crucial to delve deeper into the conservatism and comfort exhibited by boards and executive leaders, which often stems from the pressures imposed upon them by investors prioritizing quarterly profits and the pervasive fear of legal implications. Why do people live in their comfort zone?

- **Fear of Failure**. Pushing personal boundaries means taking risks. People may prefer to avoid the fear of making mistakes or experiencing setbacks.
- **Lack of Self-confidence**. Many people may lack confidence in their ability to handle new challenges or unfamiliar situations. Remaining in their comfort zone helps them maintain a sense of competence and adequacy.
- **Routine and Predictability**. Predictability can be soothing and comforting. Many prefer the stability of familiar patterns over unpredictability.

- **Fear of Judgment or Criticism.** Venturing beyond one's familiar territory can invite scrutiny or judgment from others. Some people prefer to avoid potential criticism or negative feedback, so they stay where there is less likelihood of judgment or criticism.
- **Lack of Motivation.** It takes effort and a willingness to challenge oneself. Some people lack the drive or desire to push beyond their current limits.
- **Sense of Security.** People can seek familiarity and stability to create a sense of safety and security. They prefer familiar environments and routines rather than taking risks that could potentially disrupt their sense of security.
- **Conditioning and Habit.** Human beings are creatures of habit, and it can be challenging to break free from established routines and behaviors. Some people prefer their comfort zone simply because it has become a deeply ingrained pattern of thought and behavior. It requires effort and willingness to overcome this condition and embrace new experiences.

If you truly desire personal growth, it's crucial to step out of your comfort zone. It's in this uncharted territory that life truly begins. Sadly, many people choose the illusion of comfort over the freedom of growth. Despite their unhappiness with current circumstances, they prefer to remain stagnant rather than take a leap of faith into the unknown. But it's precisely in the face of discomfort that we discover unique strengths and unleash the power to become a better version of ourselves.

Consequences of Living in the Comfort Zone

Irons rusts from disuse, stagnant water loses its purity and in cold weather becomes frozen; even so does inaction sap the vigor of the mind.

–Leonardo da Vinci[25]

---

[25] Leonardo da Vinci, *The Notebooks of Leonardo da Vinci,* [Volume] *I: Prolegomena and General Introduction to the Book on Painting*, 1883.

Living life in safe spaces leads to mental complacency, where it's difficult to experience personal growth and development. Staying within safe boundaries means we tend to stick to familiar routines and avoid taking risks or trying new things. This hampers self-improvement, learning, and exploring new opportunities. In any organization, some people spend years in the same job or a series of similar jobs. They come to work every morning and perform the work required. Their days are busy and full of activity, and they go home at the end of the day. The cycle repeats itself daily until the weekend arrives. They need to rest and relax because they worked hard all week.

Organizations often prioritize stability and incremental progress rather than embracing disruptive changes. I have found that employees consistently exhibit untapped potential and a desire for continuous growth. It's the work environment that either fosters or inhibits their willingness to take risks and explore their bolder selves. To create such an environment, a disruptive leader must possess a high level of empathy, recognize and understand the human aspect of their employees, gain their trust, and inspire their belief in what is possible. Organizational environments and culture often force them to enter a "robotic mode" where they are little more than mechanical people, repeating the tasks programmed into them, even though they have huge potential to do more.

This causes mental complacency and becomes a problem because their knowledge rarely extends beyond what they knew when they were first hired. Either they learn very slowly or not at all. Mental complacency occurs when people do not have access to a steady stream of new knowledge or information and when they are not exposed to different viewpoints, new perspectives, or new people. They may subconsciously tell themselves, "Hey, I go to work. I do my job and work hard, then go home. Why do I need to learn?"

Mental complacency occurs when people do not see the need to learn. "If I learn something, if I do things differently, if I put myself in a different situation, what would it mean to my status quo? Would it create a challenge for me?" This is a subconscious conversation that people have with themselves. Once a person is firmly entrenched in their comfort zone, they feel no need to advance and, therefore, just stop learning. Many disadvantages come from living in your comfort zone, including the following:

- **Limited Experiences**. We limit ourselves to a narrow range of experiences and miss out on new adventures, exciting challenges, and opportunities for personal and professional development. This can result in a stagnant and monotonous life.
- **Missed Opportunities**. Growth and success often comes from stepping outside of our comfort zone and taking on new challenges. By clinging to the familiar and avoiding risks, we miss valuable opportunities for learning, advancement, and personal fulfilment. This can lead to regret and a sense of unfulfilled potential.
- **Lack of Resilience**. Being unable to push the boundaries leaves us ill-equipped to handle unexpected changes or setbacks. By avoiding challenges and risks, we do not develop the resilience and adaptability necessary to navigate life's difficulties. This can make it harder to cope with change and hinder personal development.
- **Limited Self-confidence**. Stepping outside of our safe space and successfully facing challenges boosts our self-confidence and self-esteem. Conversely, living in the comfort zone can result in self-doubt and a lack of belief in our own abilities. This can hold us back from pursuing our goals and reaching our full potential.
- **Regret and Missed Growth Opportunities**. As time passes, being unwilling to leave the comfort zone leads to feelings of regret and a sense of unfulfillment. Looking back, we realize that we played it safe and missed opportunities to grow, learn, and achieve meaningful experiences. This can create a sense of longing for what could have been.

It's important to remember that while your comfort zone provides a sense of security, personal growth, and fulfillment lie within reach just beyond its boundaries. Stepping outside your boundaries brings new perspectives, accomplishments, and a greater sense of self-confidence.

You cannot chase safety and count on emptying yourself of your best work. You cannot pursue greatness and comfort at the same time. Commit today to stepping outside your comfort zone and set some goals to help you get there. In short, grow.

—Todd Henry (emphasis in the original)[26]

I believe that staying within your comfort zone leads to mediocrity. Contrary to popular belief, mediocrity does not necessarily indicate a state of underperformance. Rather, it resides on a continuum in one's mindset. It signifies a surrender to inertia, a state of contentment in the middle ground. Etymologically, *mediocrity* originates from two Latin words, *medius*, denoting the middle, and *ocris*, representing a rugged mountain. Essentially, it describes the act of settling at the halfway point of a formidable peak. It symbolizes a compromise between one's aptitudes and potential, a delicate negotiation between the pursuit of excellence and the innate inclination to seek comfort within familiar territories.

I have witnessed firsthand how organizations (some of which were once well-known brands) become obsolete when their leaders clung to old ways—mediocrity—and resisted change. They say, "Well, this is the way we've done it for the last fifty years. It works, we're making money, why change?" Because society, technology, and almost everything else around you are changing!

This attitude is dangerous, as some major companies have found that their businesses are no longer competitive or viable. Instead of making copious amounts of profit, as they did for many years, their executives are "retiring," and thousands of

---

[26] Todd Henry, *Die Empty: Unleash Your Best Work Every Day*. New York City: Penguin Random House, 2013.

their former employees are heading for the unemployment lines! It does not have to be so.

Since 2000, 52% of companies in the Fortune 500 have either gone bankrupt, been acquired, or ceased to exist. US corporations in the S&P 500 in 1958 remained in the index for an average of 61 years. By 1980, the average tenure of an S&P 500 firm was 25 years, and by 2011, that average shortened to 18 years based on seven-year rolling averages. These are challenging times for companies as the speed, volume, and complexity of change intensify.

–Capgemini Consulting[27]

One critical factor that contributes to these failures is the reluctance of established leaders to comprehend and adapt to the changing times. They often find themselves trapped in a dangerous sense of contentment, residing in a comfort zone that hinders progress. This complacency, marked by a false sense of security and misplaced confidence leads them to believe that change is unnecessary when things are going well. It raises a perplexing question: how can highly intelligent individuals from reputed institutions with decades of industry experience go from success to oblivion seemingly overnight?

While there may be multiple factors at play, one crucial yet often overlooked element is *leadership failure*. These leaders persist in outdated ways, refusing to embrace change and clinging to familiar routines until it's too late. A culture and organizational focus on short-term gains hinder efforts to shape long-term business strategies. Innovation and diversity become secondary considerations, deemed unnecessary for already successful companies. Those who prioritize short-term objectives are rewarded handsomely, while the long-term sustainability of the company hangs in the balance.

---

[27] Capgemini Consulting, "When Digital Disruption Strikes: How Can Incumbents Respond?" Paris: Capgemini Consulting, 2015. Read the full report at: https://www.capgemini.com/consulting/wp-content/uploads/sites/30/2017/07/digital_disruption_1.pdf, accessed 24 February 2024.

These leaders maintain the status quo, surround themselves with like-minded individuals, encourage cronyism, and resist the inclusion of disruptive thinkers. Consequently, when disruption strikes, they find themselves ill-prepared to respond, often abandoning ship with lucrative severance packages, leaving a wake of unemployed employees in their path. In today's world, the prevalence of such leaders has grown exponentially, spanning across all companies and industries. As conventional wisdom and outdated leadership models falter and as disruptive forces render old rules of the game obsolete, new rules emerge to shape the future. It's precisely this reason that compelled me to write this book—to ignite within these leaders the motivation to embrace disruption.

What has brought them this far will not necessarily suffice to propel them further.

Challenging the Comfort Zone Head-On

The main difference between those who disrupt and those who are disrupted is their dependence on comfort.

—Juanita Vorster[28]

Dealing with the Fear of Failure

Fear of failure is the biggest barrier that keeps people in their comfort zone. Dealing with my fear of failure has been a journey. I began by understanding that failure is a natural part of growth and learning. I challenged myself by setting small, achievable goals outside my comfort zone and gradually increased the difficulty. This is no different from embracing an exercise routine where you gradually increase the level of exercise every few weeks. Embracing a growth mindset helped me view failures as opportunities for improvement

---

[28] Juanita Vorster, "Risking for Reward," *Skyways* (Airlink's in-flight magazine). Midrand, South Africa: Panorama Media Corp., April 2023.

and learning. With each step, I gained confidence, expanded my comfort zone, and discovered new potential within myself.

For instance, why do some companies neglect innovation? Similarly, the unaddressed potential of cognitive and cultural diversity in leadership begs the question—why have these known benefits not been fully harnessed? And what about the diversification of supply chains to mitigate risks—why do some organizations still shy away from it? Could it be a fear of failure, a reluctance to invest for long-term benefit, the management's apprehension about hiring individuals who may outshine their own capabilities, or that the existing power structure might get disrupted? These are all important considerations.

Problem-Solving Rather than Problem-Thinking

In the realm of problem-solving, I have undergone a significant mindset shift over the years. Rather than fixating on the problem, I now strive to uncover creative solutions. It's challenging to avoid becoming consumed by negativity, especially in situations where people feel they are unfairly treated. But instead of dwelling on perceived injustices and getting into a negative frame of mind, I learned to address unproductive thoughts and embrace a proactive approach. I remind myself that every problem has a hidden solution awaiting discovery. I just need to change my attitude and perspective. Embracing a solution-oriented mindset empowers me to tackle obstacles with greater effectiveness and creativity. I find solace in knowing that within each problem lies an opportunity for growth and enlightenment.

Making Difficult Decisions

Many managers will not make decisions if they are outside what makes them feel comfortable. Making difficult decisions can be daunting, but there are a few strategies that helped me navigate through these situations. First, I acknowledged my fears and self-doubt but reminded myself that growth and opportunities lie beyond my comfort zone. I gathered as much information as possible about the situation, sought different perspectives, and looked at potential outcomes.

Next, I evaluated the potential risks and rewards, weighed the possibilities, considered the long-term impact, and informed relevant stakeholders. Finally, I trusted my intuition and took that leap of faith, knowing that even if the decision didn't turn out as expected, I would learn and grow from the experience and process. I also kept everyone impacted by my decisions informed and ensured they were on the journey right beside me.

Conquering Mental Barriers

Mental barriers are another reason why people do not push their boundaries. This can be due to limited knowledge and reluctance to learn more. There are many examples where managers with serious mental barriers have jeopardized the success of their businesses. Corporate culture also plays a role in people conquering mental barriers. Dealing with mental barriers to expand my comfort zone has been a critical part of my leadership journey.

First, I became self-aware, and I acknowledged and accepted the presence of these barriers, whether they stemmed from fear, self-doubt, or limiting beliefs.

Second, I consciously challenged these thoughts by questioning their validity and reframing them into more empowering beliefs. I sought support from mentors, friends, or peers who could offer guidance and encouragement. Finally, I took small, deliberate steps outside my comfort zone and celebrated each achievement along the way.

Constructive Dissatisfaction Is Critical

At the core of leading a fulfilling life lies a profound balance between gratitude and discontent. Dissatisfaction is not born out of trivial whining or ingratitude. It arises from a genuine yearning for personal growth and transformation, so it's constructive dissatisfaction.

In my encounters with high-impact leaders, I have witnessed the allure of perpetual evolution. These individuals continuously strive for more and never settle for the status quo. An unwavering commitment to growth marks the most enthralling journeys. Without actively pursuing personal development, we risk becoming trapped in an endless cycle of monotony, merely existing rather than truly living. The passage of time alone does not guarantee meaningful progress. It's the deliberate pursuit of growth that holds the key to a truly profound and fulfilling existence.

Upskilling Every Day

Upskilling has proven to be an effective way to expand my comfort zone. By acquiring new knowledge and developing new skills, I push myself to step outside familiar territory. It allows me to embrace new challenges and opens doors to new opportunities. You can upskill by seeking out interesting people and being inquisitive, which unlocks something that can then drive you into disruptive change. Upskilling boosts my confidence and equips me with the tools to tackle unfamiliar tasks with more ease. It empowers me to take on new responsibilities, broaden my horizons, and expand my comfort zone.

Embracing Emerging Technologies and Artificial Intelligence

In today's rapidly evolving technological landscape, it has become increasingly crucial for companies to venture out of their comfort zones and embrace emerging technologies to stay competitive. One such technologies making waves across industries is generative artificial intelligence (GenAI). Companies that fail to recognize and adapt to this transformative force may face existential crises over the next decade.

GenAI refers to the ability of machines to autonomously create and generate new content, such as images, music, videos, or even entire narratives, that mimic human-like creativity. This technology has the potential to revolutionize various sectors, including marketing, entertainment, design, healthcare, and more. Companies that recognize this potential and actively integrate GenAI into their operations will have a significant advantage, while those that hesitate or resist may find themselves struggling to survive.

The use of GenAI can unlock new avenues for innovation and development. By leveraging this technology, companies can push the boundaries of what is possible, fueling creativity and problem-solving. Companies that fail to harness the power of GenAI risk falling behind their competitors. With the potential to disrupt and reshape industries, early adopters of this technology will likely gain significant market share and customer loyalty. In contrast, companies resistant to change may find themselves struggling to keep up with evolving customer demands, losing market relevance, and even facing the risk of obsolescence.

To overcome these formidable challenges, companies must break free from their comfort zones and adopt a comprehensive approach to evaluating their performance. Striking a delicate balance between short-term gains and long-term adaptability is crucial to meet the ever-changing demands of clients and markets. While easier said than done, fortunate individuals such as myself have had the privilege of working alongside exceptional leaders at GHD and KPMG, leaders who have successfully achieved this crucial equilibrium. These industry visionaries are invaluable examples of resilience and foresight. Their stories serve as beacons of hope, inspiring companies to navigate the treacherous waters of change with strength and forward thinking.

It is imperative for companies to understand that the old parameters of success no longer align with the new expectations in today's dynamic landscape. If organizations wish to do more than survive and if they wish to thrive, then they must critically assess their culture and leadership capabilities. Will these leaders guide them into the future or simply reap the benefits when things are going well?

Managing Ego

In the realm of large organizations, the human ego often finds fertile ground to flourish and expand. It's an intriguing phenomenon that sometimes the size of one's title or team seems to directly correlate with the magnitude of their ego.

As individuals climb the hierarchical ladder, there is a tendency for power and authority to inflate their sense of self-importance. The allure of a prestigious position or status in the organization can subtly distort their perception, leading them to believe they are somehow superior to their colleagues and subordinates. I once had a senior executive declare to me, "I am God." At first, I thought he was joking, but he was not. I also frequently see individuals at senior levels grossly exaggerate their capabilities and past experiences just to feed their egos, as if they have new interpretations of reality.

This inflated ego can manifest in arrogance, a dismissive attitude toward others' opinions, and an insatiable hunger for recognition and validation.

It's crucial to understand that ego, in and of itself, is not inherently negative. It plays a vital role in shaping individuality and propelling us toward success, achievement, and personal growth. However, when ego becomes inflated, it blinds us to our shortcomings, manifests as arrogance, obstructs effective collaboration, and hinders progress. Since my early days as a student of philosophy, I have developed a deep desire to understand the intricacies of ego in our personal and professional lives. In pursuit of this understanding, I've delved into the works of several notable individuals who have explored the concept of ego:

- **Sigmund Freud**, a famous psychologist, formulated the concept of the "ego" as part of his psychoanalytic theory. He emphasized the ego's role in mediating between the id (primitive desires) and the superego (societal norms and values).
- **Eckhart Tolle** is a spiritual teacher who discusses the ego extensively in his book *A New Earth*. He explores

how egotistic thinking and identification can lead to suffering and separation from the present moment.
- **Ryan Holiday**, an author and entrepreneur, wrote *Ego is the Enemy,* which examines the destructive nature of ego in our personal and professional lives. He explores how ego can hinder growth and success.
- **David R. Hawkins** was a psychiatrist and author who wrote *Power vs. Force,* where he discussed the concept of ego from a spiritual perspective. He proposed the idea of transcending the ego to attain higher levels of consciousness.
- **Richard Rohr**, a Franciscan friar and spiritual writer, explores the ego and its role in spiritual development in his book *Falling Upward*. He discusses how the ego must be acknowledged and transformed for true growth to occur.

These authors offer various insights into the nature of the ego and provide guidance on how to navigate its potential pitfalls.

In large organizations, where numerous individuals wield significant power, it's crucial to cultivate self-awareness and empathy. Leaders should strive to create an environment that promotes humility, open-mindedness, and collaboration. By fostering a culture that values diverse perspectives and encourages collective problem-solving, the negative repercussions of inflated egos can be mitigated. I am blessed to be working in such environments, but in the past, I have experienced the challenges of ego-driven leadership. I know what good leadership looks like and feels like. I try my best to create such an environment for my people, keeping my ego in check and seeking feedback from those willing to give candid feedback. Those of us who are willing to seek out and act on feedback find that this is an effective barrier to an out-of-control ego.

Ultimately, the focus should be on the collective welfare and success of the organization rather than the individual's ego-driven pursuit of personal gain. When individuals can set aside their egos and work toward a shared vision, the organization flourishes, and meaningful progress becomes almost certain.

Let us remember that titles and positions are mere symbols of hierarchical structure. They are valuable; they define responsibility and impose accountability, but they should never define the worth or importance of an individual. It's our actions, integrity, and empathy toward others that truly define our leadership and contribute to the growth and success of the organization as a whole.

Understanding the importance of ego, recognizing individual strengths, and fostering a collaborative environment are keys to disruptive leadership success.

Challenging My Personal Comfort Zone

Challenging the boundaries of my comfort zone has been one of the most rewarding journeys of my career. Whenever I find myself becoming complacent or stagnant, I challenge myself to explore some new opportunity. This mindset led me to leave comfortable and financially stable positions and founding a startup. Each time, I knew that staying longer would risk my growth and personal development. I also knew that living too long in my comfort zone was the beginning to the end of my leadership journey.

Venturing into entrepreneurship was a pivotal moment in my life. For many years, I faced countless challenges. It was during this time that I discovered my mental barriers, skill gaps, and mindset/attitude misalignments. This allowed me to grow and develop as an individual leader. By leaving my safe space behind, I built my startup from scratch. This allowed me to nurture my leadership skills, enhance my empathy, and increase my compassion, all of which changed me for the better.

After a few years in a startup, an opportunity to be acquired and join GHD arose. Excited by the chance to contribute to the company's goals and the opportunity to transform the industry, I joined the team, bringing a unique perspective and expertise in digital business matters to a highly successful engineering services firm with almost a hundred years of heritage.This fusion allowed us to establish a global digital business with six hundred employees over just four years. This journey was challenging beyond expectation and took me far beyond my comfort zone. It was a profound experience and reinvigorated my passion for creating something new and extraordinary.

Amidst the turbulence and challenges I faced, my journey was anything but easy. As my initiative was a driver of change, I confronted obstacles and soared through a whirlwind of emotions. In the face of adversity, I had to adapt my mindset, attitude, and approach, redefine my assumptions, and hone my communication style. It turned out to be a massive learning opportunity. The sacrifices I made to step beyond the comfort of familiarity were undoubtedly worthwhile. The sheer exhilaration of establishing a thriving global enterprise spanning nine countries surpasses anything I could have ever imagined while seeking solace in my comfort zone. My triumph over the inertia of complacency has made me a better leader and an evolved individual. I gained wisdom, experienced personal growth, and embraced an unwavering determination to learn and evolve, and that is what distinguishes me as a leader.

It's essential to push yourself outside of your comfort zone because it empowers you to change your mindset, mold your beliefs, and shape your journey through life. If you always live life in your comfort zone, nothing will change, and opportunities will pass you by.

So I invite you to step outside your comfort zone and embrace the unknown. Yes, it will be challenging and even uncomfortable at times, but the rewards are immeasurable. You will become a better leader and a better individual and shape a future that others can only dream about.

Embrace the discomfort zone, ignite your passion, and make history.

CHAPTER 5
Build Relationships That Foster Disruptive Thinking

Businesses that embrace a disruptive higher purpose tend to outperform those solely focused on maximizing profits. This has been thoroughly discussed in earlier chapters. Similarly, when companies prioritize the well-being and relationships of their employees over short-term financial gain, their employees reciprocate and put the company's best interests first.

Early in my career, I learned that the core of any organization's success lies in its people. A business, club, political party—any group—can never be better than the people who do the work for that organization. The stronger the relationships, both internally and externally (with clients, vendors, consultants, etc.), the more positive the financial and overall outcomes are for the company. Throughout my career, I have consistently witnessed the achievements of organizations that prioritize strong, positive relationships with their people. This direct correlation between healthy relationships and improved business outcomes serves as a testament to the importance of a people-centric corporate culture.

Interestingly, people from competing companies often express a desire to join our teams at GHD Digital despite the strength of their current employer's brand or strong competition for talent. Their motivation stems from a lack of fulfillment and a desire to work in an innovative, entrepreneurial, employee-centric environment where they can pursue their creative and professional potential. We managed to attract some of the best people in the industry, based on our close relationships—not only from engineering services companies, but also from leading consulting and technology firms. Some of them I had known for decades, and others were motivated by what our employees had to say. This was another proof to me of how valuable a strong and healthy relationship with people and employees truly is.

The power of relationships is demonstrated through these examples. In the early nineties, I made the transformative decision to uproot my life and settle in Australia, a land that would become my cherished home for over thirty years. Against a backdrop of modest beginnings and scarce financial resources, I embraced a newfound liberty and faced the horizon with unyielding optimism and a sense of adventure. Arriving in Australia with just five hundred dollars in my pocket, I carried with me grand dreams and ambitious aspirations.

Australia's captivating landscapes and welcoming populace swiftly captured my heart, fostering within me a deep affection for the country and its people. Despite arriving with very limited financial resources, chance encounters soon evolved into valuable connections that would reshape the course of my life. Upon enrolling at Central Queensland University, fate introduced me to five extraordinary individuals whose influence proved pivotal in shaping my journey. Thus unfolded the profound impact of disruptive relationships.

My introduction to Professor Greg Whymark marked a significant turning point. A former navy commander turned educator, Greg epitomized openness to innovation and impact. When I proposed a venture to establish a university-backed initiative for scholarships and real-world academic engagement, Greg wholeheartedly embraced the vision, leading to the inception of the Centre of Business Information Management (CBIM). Under our stewardship, CBIM flourished, providing leading-edge computer training and consultancy services to Central Queensland companies such as Stanwell Power Station, Queensland Magnesia, and Capricornia Power. Greg became my mentor and a lifelong friend, forging a bond that would endure for decades to come.

Amidst the uncertainties of my new reality, I crossed paths with the exceptional duo, Dr. Rao and Nirmala Ayyalaraju, affectionately known as "Uncle and Aunty." Hailing from my ancestral state of Andhra Pradesh and fluent in my mother tongue, Telugu, they generously extended their care and guidance, embracing me as their own son. Their unwavering love and support proved instrumental in navigating the challenges of assimilating into a foreign academic environment, providing a comforting anchor during turbulent times.

The fortuitous encounter with Peter and Sue Callaghan presented yet another opportunity for collaboration and growth. Peter, the forward-thinking general manager of CQ Personnel Services, and Sue, his efficient office manager, swiftly recognized the potential for expansion into computer training and consultancy services. Together, we harnessed our entrepreneurial spirit to pave new pathways in the Central Queensland market. The synergies between CBIM and CQ Personnel not only propelled our business endeavors but also facilitated the provision of scholarships, practical industry exposure for academics, and invaluable assistance in funding my pursuit of a master's degree in information systems.

Today, the bonds forged with the Whymarks and Callaghans endure as steadfast friendships, while my "adoptive parents," the Ayyalarajus, who live in Canberra, hold a special place in our family. The impact of these disruptive relationships is a testament to their profound influence in shaping one's destiny.

Disruptive leaders excel in expanding their networks and actively cultivating positive relationships with team members and individuals within the larger ecosystem. Some successful organizations, however, find themselves facing existential crises when they lose sight of the importance of trusted relationships and become solely focused on short-term performance. These organizations overlook the fact that stronger relationships yield better results. Instead, they rely on opportunistic and, sometimes, unethical methods to exploit their relationships for financial gain. Unsurprisingly, this short-term focus often leads to long-term trouble.

> *Positive human connection plays an important role in maintaining our emotional-physical health, well-being, and growth. Whether it be with friends, your peers, or a significant other, relationships often allow us to forge deep and meaningful bonds that can result in a sense of purpose, great joy, and satisfaction. This is primarily because of the support that comes from a healthy relationship. In the face of adversity, healthy relationships and the positive support they offer not only buffer us from the harms of stress but allow us to flourish despite these harms.*
>
> *—Stanford University*[29]

Effective networking involves nurturing meaningful human connections, both within and beyond the organization. Some of those relationships last for many years. In my case, many have continued through several decades. Strong and transparent relationships contribute not only to the growth of individuals and their teams but also to the overall success of the entire organization.

Networking and relationship building have many benefits. It's crucial to recognize that networks are increasingly valuable in everyday work, particularly as companies foster collaboration across various departments, vendors, and individuals in the gig economy.

Leaders who introduce bold, innovative ideas, products, or strategies often face resistance and skepticism from the people around them. To navigate these challenges successfully, it's crucial that disruptive leaders build a strong team that includes far-reaching relationships.

My professional experiences showed me the numerous benefits of creating a wide network of colleagues both within and outside of my employer:

---

[29] (Unbylined), "In Focus: Building and Maintaining Healthy Relationships," *StudentAffairs.Stanford.edu*. Stanford, California: Stanford University, (undated). https://studentaffairs.stanford.edu/focus-building-and-maintaining-healthy-relationships, accessed 1 February 2024.

- **Inspiring and Influencing**. As disruptive leaders, it's crucial to inspire others and rally them behind our vision for change. By nurturing strong relationships, I found we could connect with key individuals who support our ideas and help overcome resistance. These connections provide avenues to effectively communicate, persuade, and get buy-in from important stakeholders, starting with employees and sponsors.
- **Mobilizing Support and Resources**. Disruptive initiatives require resources, such as financial backing, access to talent, or support from decision-makers. Leaders can tap into a diverse pool of resources and rally support for their cause when they cultivate robust networks. For instance, when establishing our business, it was challenging to access exceptional talent, but by leveraging our personal and professional networks, we attracted top-notch individuals from our industry and adjacent industries.
- **Navigating Obstacles**. Disruptive leaders often encounter resistance from entrenched systems and traditional ways of working. Building strong relationships empowers them to navigate these obstacles more effectively. Groundbreaking ideas demand substantial change, and the relationships we build, what we sometimes call our "collaboration clusters," accelerated change by introducing new operating models, products, services, or go-to-market strategies that drive growth.
- **Fostering Collaborative Innovation**. Cross-pollination of ideas is critical for innovative leaders, especially when pioneering uncharted territories. Well-established networks help us to connect with diverse individuals and organizations to validate ideas and foster a creative environment. These connections can lead to new partnerships, joint ventures, and knowledge-sharing to drive new ideas, accelerate growth, and provide a platform for advancement.
- **Establishing Credibility and Trust**. Disruption inherently involves taking risks—venturing into the unknown—where earning credibility and trust can be very challenging. Leaders can establish themselves as

trustworthy and reliable partners through strong relationships. We enlisted key leaders from our core business teams to engage the extensive relationships they built through long tenure and experience. Leveraging the credibility of these connections combined with exceptional internal talent allowed us to gain the trust of reputable individuals. This created an easier path to trust between our innovation teams and stakeholders, which allowed us to demonstrate the potential positive impact of our disruptive initiatives. The reputation of our leaders and their connections made earning the trust of stakeholders vastly simpler.

Forward-thinking, disruptive leaders must act intentionally and deliberately to build the relationships needed to establish strong networks. This is crucial in effectively navigating challenges, gathering resources, overcoming resistance, driving collaboration and innovation, and establishing credibility. By doing so, they position themselves for success when implementing disruptive ideas and bringing meaningful change in their industries.

The Attributes of Disruptive Relationships

"Relationship" refers to any bond between two people—spouse to spouse, friend to friend, coworker to coworker, neighbor to neighbor, or any others. "Network" refers to a bond shared among a group of people—a family, a congregation, a company, or any other. I use them interchangeably because it does not matter whether it's an individual or group; the defining features of these connections are the same. They are essential for effective leadership because you influence people, you guide them, and you create a better culture through your connections. To do that, there must be mutual trust and lead by example every day. Trusting, healthy connections manifest when these happen:

- Those connected engage eagerly, communicate clearly, delegate effectively, and manage conflicts rationally.

- You believe in other people, and they believe in you. Everyone trusts that no one is going to take advantage of anyone else.
- You and they grow as a direct result of your connection. This could be financial growth, individual advancement, or organizational progress. The stronger the relationships, the more productive the outcomes.
- We act for each other's benefit. Each project needs a definable profit, and, when all is said and done, each person in the relationship or network can identify the profit they've achieved through that activity.
- You respect others for who they are and what they can do, and they respect you for your character and skills.
- You value teamwork and safety. You work together in a synergistic environment where risks are shared (eliminated, if possible), and so are the rewards. No teamwork, no success.
- You seek a personal, as well as an organizational, connection—shared common interests, hobbies, family events, and social events, and you grow to care about them as people, not just as steppingstones to success.

I've been fortunate to develop close relationships with my team leaders, peers, and superiors, men and women who are incredibly successful individuals managing multimillion-dollar and sometimes multibillion-dollar businesses. These relationships have allowed me to challenge them in ways that others could not, and they do the same because we have trusted relationships. Whether it's about values, the direction of the business, or their interactions with their teams and clients, they trust that my intentions are in their best interest and respond in kind.

Trust is the foundation that enables leaders to inspire and motivate their people. Without trust, it's challenging to truly influence and convince others to believe what you say.

Networking is vital because no leader can accomplish everything alone or has all the answers. Strong networks allow us to call on others to achieve organizational goals. A network built on mutual trust can provide invaluable resources that may not be accessible otherwise. I've invested time and effort into nurturing relationships with senior executives, community leaders, and government officials. These connections have opened doors to many successful individuals. The trust my friends and I have within our networks gives us access to resources and expertise to address challenges and needs. In addition, cultivating relationships with the youth and individuals from diverse cultural backgrounds plays a significant role in nurturing talent.

Building trust and cultivating personal relationships takes time and effort. Rather than striving for thousands of superficial connections, I believe in creating a cluster of a small number trusted relationships over a few years. These focus on specific goals or projects and are characterized by deep connection, mutual respect, shared values, and the potential for personal and professional growth, and that is the differentiating factor.

This ancient proverb still holds true: "Ye help me, and I help thee, and together we shall rise." It's a simple but powerful precept. Building trust and networks based on genuine support and collaboration will always yield success and growth.

Common Myths

The organizational environment and leadership have a different impact on relationship building. Often, the focus is on sales, operations, products, or services that are routine training. There is little emphasis on relationships. Over time, I discovered many leadership myths and misconceptions that can hinder a leader's effectiveness and limit their potential to build strong relationships with their team. Let us understand ten of the myths a little better:

Leaders Should Always Have the Answers

An old sage once suggested, "Good leaders do not need to have all the answers. They don't even need to have all the questions. They need to know how to *find* the right questions and who has the right answers." They should encourage open communication and collaboration within the team to find the best solutions together. Admitting you do not know something actually builds trust and fosters a culture of continuous learning. I often say, "I don't have an answer to this challenge, but I am confident we will collectively find one."

Leaders Must Display Strength; Asking for Help Is a Sign Of Weakness

Leaders often feel compelled to maintain an image of strength and competence, fearing that any admission of weakness may undermine their authority. However, recognizing and addressing weaknesses also fosters trust and authenticity within the team. Sharing struggles and soliciting input from others promotes collaboration, problem-solving, and personal growth. It's important to remember that no leader possesses expertise in every area, and thinking that asking for help is a sign of weakness only limits personal and organizational development.

Leaders Must Always Be in Control

The leader is, by definition, responsible for the team, but great leaders balance control and empowerment. Micromanaging—looking over people's shoulders, as we used to say—harms relationships with team members. Instead, effective leaders trust them to take ownership of their work and only provide guidance and support as needed. Giving employees autonomy and empowering them leads to increased motivation, creativity, and a stronger sense of ownership. Another aspect of excessive control is taking credit for other people's work. A good leader never fails to heap praise on his or her team members because they understand, "My people's successes are also my successes, and mine are theirs."

Leaders Must Always Be Certain

"Leader" does not mean "fearless." Acknowledging and addressing one's fears openly creates a supportive environment where team members feel comfortable discussing their concerns. Effective leaders are willing to take risks and face challenges while also recognizing their limitations and seeking input from their teams.

This is not limited to the challenges of the project. A team member with a seriously ill child, for example, is a distracted worker who isn't putting out their best effort. Support from the team can't solve that problem, but it can make the whole situation less tense and less frightening, which, for anyone who's been through such trauma, is priceless.

Leaders Must Always Be Charismatic and Extroverted

While charisma is an asset, effective leadership is not limited to extroverts. Good leaders can possess a range of personality traits and leadership styles as long as they focus on understanding and meeting the needs of their team members. Listening actively, fostering inclusivity, and adapting their approach to different individuals builds strong relationships. As long as they see you are trying to be the best leader you can be, they will respond positively.

Challenges and Questions from the Team Diminish a Leader's Authority and Respect

Leaders may mistakenly believe that they can only earn respect through authority and avoiding dissent. However, respect is more likely to be fostered in an environment that encourages open dialogue and healthy debate. Allowing your team to challenge your ideas and decisions gives them a sense of ownership and autonomy, leading to better engagement and commitment. Remember the proverb, "If both always agree, one of you is unnecessary."

It's Lonely at the Top; Leaders Cannot Allow People to Get Too Close

It has been axiomatic that leaders distance themselves emotionally from their team and maintain a sense of isolation. That idea has long since been proven false in almost every situation. Effective leadership requires building strong connections among team members. Being close to your people helps create trust and understanding, fostering collaboration. Collaboration leads to increased team morale and productivity. Leaders must also draw a clear line, never disclosing matters that require confidentiality and discretion in the name of "open communication."

Leaders Must Keep Their Personal and Professional Lives Separate

Many leaders believe that discussing their personal lives can undermine their professional image or create biases. However, sharing appropriate aspects of your personal life humanizes you as a leader and fosters deeper connections with your team members. The best way to build close friendships at work is to share commonalities. Chances are high that children of several team members play on school sports teams or participate in other similar activities or that team members share hobbies. A "no work discussed" monthly lunch might be a very simple way to allow team members to share family news and achievements that can be celebrated by all. It's one of many simple ways to create a positive work environment where everyone feels valued.

Leaders Must Build Relationships with Everyone

Although it's often suggested to forge connections with anyone possible, this approach is generally not efficient. In the business environment, a lack of selectivity can potentially waste time. In truth, you never know who might be of value to your initiatives someday. However, constructing relationships demands emotional energy and time, both of which must be spent wisely. I advocate prioritizing our focus on identifying individuals who can contribute to our vision or mission. Enlisting the wrong people can even hinder progress.

Everyone Should Love the Leader

This notion is not realistic or feasible, especially when leaders are required to make difficult decisions. In such situations, leaders must consider the greater good of the organization over personal popularity, which can result in displeasure or disagreement from certain individuals. Effective leaders understand the importance of making tough calls, even if it means not being universally liked, and, instead, focus on maintaining trust, respect, and open communication with their teams.

Leaders must understand these myths and why they're false and address them to foster profitable relationships, effective communication, and a supportive work environment.

Disruptive Relationships Are Catalysts for Personal Growth

Using trusted relationships for personal growth involves leveraging the support, guidance, and feedback of the people who are close to you and have your best interests at heart.

The importance of relationships is backed up by research. Studies show that social connections play a central role in fostering a sense of purpose and well-being in the workplace. T hey also impact the bottom line: Effective management of social capital within organizations facilitates learning and knowledge sharing, increases employee retention and engagement, reduces burnout, sparks innovation, and improves employee and organizational performance.

–Rob Cross[30]

I've found several practices by which my relationships have assisted in my personal growth:

- **Seek Honest Feedback**. Approach trusted connections and ask for constructive criticism or feedback. This helps you identify areas for improvement and means for improvement.

---

[30] Rob Cross, "To Be Happier at Work Invest More in Your Relationships," *Harvard Business Review*. Brighton, Massachusetts: Harvard Business Publishing, 30 July 2019.

- **Share Goals**. Communicate your personal aspirations with the people you trust. They can provide valuable insights, advice, and support to help you achieve them.
- **Learn from Their Experiences**. Tap into the wisdom of your trusted connections. Seek their guidance and advice when faced with new challenges or difficult decisions. Their perspectives may provide insight and meaningful lessons.
- **Engage in Open Conversations**. Foster honest conversations with the people you trust. Discuss topics that are important to you and explore different viewpoints and ideas. If you know they speak with your best interest at heart, you can be confident their advice is meant to help you be a better person, broaden your perspective, or facilitate your personal growth.
- **Immerse Yourself in Positive Influences**. Surround yourself with individuals who uplift and inspire you. The power of positive relationships is immeasurable as they possess the ability to ignite personal growth, serving as catalysts that consistently motivate and empower you to reach for unparalleled excellence.
- **Collaborate and Learn Together**. Engage in activities with people you trust. This could involve pursuing shared hobbies, attending workshops or courses together, or brainstorming ideas. Collaborative efforts strengthen connections, build trust, enhance growth, foster understanding, and aid in personal development—yours and theirs.
- **Lean on Them during Challenging Times**. During times of adversity or struggle, rely on your connections for support and encouragement. Sharing your difficulties allows them to provide emotional support and a fresh perspective. If they can't improve your situation, the fact that you know people you can count on, even just for a listening ear, can be the difference between overcoming and being overwhelmed.

One of the most impactful professional relationships I had was with Ashley Wright, the Global CEO of GHD and my boss for many years. Ashley excelled at balancing short-term and long-term goals with unmatched skill among senior leaders.

The mutual challenges we engaged in, approached with open-mindedness and a spirit of radical candor, significantly propelled my personal development and learning. Our collaboration became a crucial catalyst for the establishment of GHD Digital and my growth, nurturing my professional skills and shaping me as an individual.

My personal growth has been a continuous journey, and my trusted connections have played a significant role in guiding, supporting, and inspiring me along the way. It'll be the same for you.

Trusted Relationships Allow Robust Conversations

It's crucial to engage in robust discussion to achieve success, particularly in the context of disruptive opportunities. "Robust" conversations are vigorous, substantive, passionate, respectful, and focused on answers. Even in relationships where there is a close bond and genuine caring for one another, it's necessary to challenge one another. Shared values and alignment do not guarantee agreement on every issue. Nothing does. However, different perspectives can still contribute to the same goal. It's like standing on railroad tracks. The rails may seem separate at your feet but come together in the distance. Mutual respect, in the form of negotiation and compromise, brings divergent thoughts or plans together to reach a common destination.

In my trusted relationships, we often have intense discussions that may appear as arguments to outsiders. We passionately debate and sometimes agree to disagree, always returning to what is best for our common purpose. These spirited debates indicate the trust and respect we have for each other. In some of my closest relationships, we engage in discussions and openly express disagreement or suggest alternative actions. We prioritize open and direct dialogue, knowing that we all have the same end goal in mind.

I appreciate it and consider myself lucky when someone challenges my thinking and asks for more information.

Rather than viewing it as an insult, I see good banter, healthy disagreement, and learning from each other as essential in our interactions. Though we may become heated at times due to passion for our positions, we always return to our underlying trust. Robust discussions end with a plan that we can all support. I believe professionals should regularly have robust discussions about everything involved in their projects and goals.

Disruptive leadership involves fostering a collaborative environment where questions are answered and challenges are met. We must challenge the status quo and encourage critical and creative thinking among our staff, colleagues, and leaders. To achieve this, it's important to create a safe space for constructive dialogue and radical candor.

I am known for promoting individuals who approach their managers and propose alternative ways of thinking. I even hold competitions with small token prizes to promote constructive challenges and new thinking. Constructive challenges to the status quo must be rewarded rather than punished. By asking open-ended questions and encouraging diverse perspectives, we can drive enriching discussions and innovative solutions. It's crucial to challenge assumptions and conventional wisdom, questioning why things need to be done in a certain way.

Vulnerability Is a Strength

It takes tremendous strength to express vulnerability and you need a lot of courage and strength to be vulnerable.

–Simon Sinek[31]

---

[31] Simon Sinek, *Encourage Vulnerability* (video). New York City: The Optimism Company, (undated). The full presentation reposted at: https://www.linkedin.com/posts/manju-abraham_it-takes-tremendous-courage-to-be-able-to-activity-7062623238207520768-9XZN, accessed 24 February 2024.

Many of us grew up in a business culture where vulnerability was often equated with a lack of ability or weakness. Leaders were taught to be strong in every situation. The ideas "Real men don't cry" and "Women are too emotional" are equally idiotic. Only recently has vulnerability become a desirable attribute for authentic leadership.

In our living memory, there were dictators to beat—Stalin, Mao, Tojo—and heroes—General McArthur and Field Marshall Montgomery—who beat them. Scientists, athletes, and even businesspeople joined that Pantheon, and we never looked at their flaws. No one ever mentioned that Churchill and Mickey Mantle were alcoholics. Still, no one listens when Ronald Reagan's children describe his failures as a father. It was all hushed up because great men and women were bulletproof; they could walk on water and bring victory from certain defeat—they were a combination of John Wayne and Mother Theresa. And once we had television, they did all that in forty-six minutes plus commercials.

Gradually, the world began to publicly recognize that all humans are imperfect, and gradually, I learned to be more vulnerable to the people I trusted, more so during COVID. There has been a long overdue shift in the human expectations of our leaders. This has come about partly because leadership has become more of an emotional than a business exercise because business is no longer just about the bottom-line quarterly profit statement. It's about emotional connection to stakeholders and the planet. Because we spend so much time at work, what we do there impacts all aspects of our lives as well as our communities, societies, and the world.

In the post-COVID era, the world expects leaders to be more genuine, authentic, and empathetic—more like parents than drill sergeants. Leaders need to recognize their weaknesses, share them with team members, and allow team member's strengths to complement their weaknesses. This is one key to creating synergy.

One of my weaknesses is a lack of patience. Another is my tendency not to listen as actively as I should. I am gradually becoming more patient and a better listener, and both efforts have been made easier by understanding and supportive coworkers. As I progress in my journey of self-improvement, I share some of these things with my team members and their trust in me increases.

The disruptive leader is far from infallible, devoid of any superhuman abilities. There are no miracle workers or superheroes—just ordinary individuals continuously learning and collaboratively cultivating trust among team members.

Over time, the work team should become your friends, and with time, they become like family. My actual family may hear from me daily, and my work team almost rivals that frequency. At peak business times, I must spend more time at work than at home. I maintain open lines of communication with both, constantly planning and executing activities and relying on others for collective success. Coworkers are privy to my strengths and weaknesses and, likewise, share their own daily experiences. Trust is an essential cornerstone, mutually deserved, and bestowed upon both parties. Embracing vulnerability yields a direct benefit, fostering candor and trust among my team, ultimately improving communication and engagement with all stakeholders.

Situations arise that can compromise a person's effectiveness but can be covered by a little extra effort by others. For example, anybody can face a health situation. We all have our fears and demons. One young professional talked to me about "imposter syndrome"–the feeling that their success is a mistake. I said, "Look, I had that fear as well. It's not just a problem women deal with. I've faced that, and I dealt with it, and I dealt with it in this way." Maybe that advice was exactly what was needed; maybe it helped just to know somebody else felt it and got through it. Either way, it brought us together, improved communication and our ability to connect, and boosted their confidence, knowing they were not alone.

Vulnerability also allows you to learn and improve. For example, when I realized and acknowledged I had to become a better active listener a few years back, people reached out to me. "Kumar, you're thinking of improving your listening skills. This article about active listening may be very good for you. Have a look at it; maybe you'll find something useful." Becoming open about vulnerability has been good for my personal growth as well as for nurturing a culture of change and innovation in all the organizations I have been a part of.

Successful leaders acknowledge their limitations and actively seek guidance and support from others. Embracing diverse perspectives and leveraging the strengths of the team can lead to better decisions and innovative solutions. Admitting your vulnerabilities is one mark of strong leadership.

Breakdown the Walls

Connecting to other individuals and teams isn't the only challenge in disruptive leadership. Many teams and companies are challenged by other outmoded ideals:

- **Short-termism**. A major barrier to creating disruptive relationships is short-term thinking. When individuals or organizations focus on personal or short-term gains, they cannot visualize the future. They are less likely to invest in building strong, lasting relationships. This may include making choices that maximize current benefits that leave long-term unfavorable consequences for others, which can hinder the development of trust, collaboration, and innovation, and lead to unsustainable relationships.
- **Cultural Barriers.** Cultural barriers can impede the establishment of disruptive relationships. Differences in values, beliefs, and practices across cultures can create misunderstandings, communication gaps, and conflicts. Overcoming cultural barriers requires open-mindedness, cultural competence, and a willingness to adapt and bridge the gaps in understanding.

Organizations should create an internal culture that encourages the development of deep relationships.
- **Unhealthy Competition**. Healthy competition is valuable; it drives quality and can be made fun. Unhealthy competition among individuals or entities poses a significant barrier to disruptive relationships. Executives at senior levels compete with each other to the detriment of their teams. When the focus is solely on outperforming others or gaining an internal competitive advantage, it can negatively affect collaboration and cooperation. It's important to shift the mindset from a zero-sum game mentality to a win-win approach that fosters mutual benefit.
- **High-Tech Dependency**. While technology has greatly facilitated communication and connection, it can also become a barrier to creating disruptive relationships when overused. Reliance on technology, such as email, virtual meetings, or social media platforms, leads to a lack of genuine human connections and hinders building trust and meaningful relationships.
- **Treating People Like Commodities**. Viewing individuals as a means to an end rather than as valued partners is a significant barrier to disruptive relationships. When people are treated as commodities, their unique perspectives, skills, and contributions are undervalued, which creates an environment discouraging collaboration, innovation, and the establishment of meaningful relationships. Empathy is a common weakness of highly ambitious people.

Breaking down these walls requires a shift in mindset and focusing on long-term goals. It's important to foster a culture of collaboration and inclusivity, balance healthy competition and technology usage, and recognize the value of individuals as people.

Relationships and networks built on trust are vital. You cannot achieve disruption alone. You can leverage these connections to open doors to people you may not have met yet and give you access to valuable resources that may not be accessible otherwise. It's important to invest time in cultivating relationships with a broad selection of individuals. When you share values and respect with others, you grow professionally and personally.

CHAPTER 6
Disrupt the Status Quo

Here's a short lesson in Latin:

- *Status quo* (literally, "the existing state") refers to the current state of affairs and the way things are today.
- *Stare decisis* (literally, "to stand by a decision") is a legal term in which cases are decided based on precedent—what other judges have decided in the past.
- *Torpor* (literally, "complacency") describes an attitude of apathy, lethargy, idleness, even laziness.

Those studying this book should already know what these almost-forgotten terms have to do with disruptive leadership:

Status quo plus *stare decisis* equals *torpor*.

To be fair, there are upsides to each of these ideas:

- We, humans find comfort and security in stability, and businesses can turn routines into money-saving, efficient methods.
- Laws that do not change on a judge's whim are the foundations of a fair and equitable justice system.
- To live your life in a state of restlessness often leads to unnecessary stress.

However, when people decide to continue doing things the same way because they don't believe they can do better than others have done in the past, we're dead. Stagnation sets in. When our way of living and doing business reaches a set-in-stone state of mind, people and businesses may go years without any significant improvement in their situation. In the twenty-first century, an era defined so far by unrelenting change, the importance of disrupting the status quo cannot be overstated. The corporate landscape is undergoing a transformative revolution, with digital giants reshaping industries and traditional titans falling by the wayside. Gone are the days of relying on past successes or clinging to outdated models.

In this rapidly evolving environment, survival belongs to those who embrace agility and innovation, while others face the looming threat of irrelevance.

What sets true disruptive leaders apart from others? Is it access to immense capital or cutting-edge technology? While these factors certainly play a role, a hidden force often goes unnoticed—the power of radical thinking, the courage to question conventions, and the ability to envision what others consider implausible. Delving deeper into this realm, we uncover the secret weapon that catapults businesses to new heights and dismantles industry giants—the unparalleled potential of creative thought. In this journey, we explore how creative thinking transcends being merely an asset and how it serves as the lifeblood of disrupting the status quo of modern businesses.

While it may be tempting to bask in the comforts of familiarity, doing so within the dynamic world of business can prove costly. Clinging to well-trodden paths and established practices may offer temporary solace but often lead to stagnation and hinder long-term growth and sustainability. Such complacency and resistance to change blind companies to emerging trends, evolving customer needs, and revolutionary technologies. Consequently, what was once an industry leader can swiftly descend into obsolescence—a stark reminder of the perils of dismissing the call for transformation.

The status quo is valuable if it forms the baseline of your actions. Your year-to-year baseline should be where you start. Then you must consider how you need to move to reflect changes in society, regulations, culture, and economics. Last year is the starting point from which changes and improvements can be decided, planned, executed, and measured so that you can reach where you want and need to be next year.

I believe that stare decisis is valuable. We need to respect what has gone before; it's the foundation of what we have achieved. It, too, forms a baseline. We know we can do this much, so let us examine every aspect of our work and let it inspire us to improve.

Torpor is inevitable. Humans do not naturally want to put in more effort than necessary. That threat should motivate us to keep a watchful eye on who we are and what we do and inspire us to do better. Humans also naturally want something better. We need to work at making the motivation for something better and stronger than our inclination to sit back and just get by.

Why Do People Like to Maintain the Status Quo?

Disruptive leaders seeking to be change agents can be challenged by the way their organization operates.

Organizations may have a proven successful recipe that has worked efficiently and profitably for a very long time. They may, as a result, believe that their recipe will continue to work for them for the foreseeable future. What they may not realize is that external changes—in technology, culture, consumer preferences, in any one of a hundred other things—will sink their success plan like a rock.

Hierarchy

The hierarchy comprises those individuals who sit in the center chairs. It's often called the "powers-that-be" or the "establishment"—the people with real control over a company. They make the decisions that trickle down and impact all employees. If the hierarchy is not thinking about the ever-changing market and changing its products to meet new market demands, sell your stock quickly!

They can slow down or even stop a disruptive leader trying to change the status quo. This can happen because they are not familiar with (or maybe even aware of) new ways of doing things. This generally happens because they are satisfied doing what works. After all, it has worked for a long time, so they stopped looking for ways to do it better. Alternately, they may resist change because they want to hang on to power, and changing the status quo may dilute the power between the old and the new leadership.

Bureaucracy

People may say, "Oh, yes, we have to change. We have to move into the future." Then they proceed to build an organizational structure that will supposedly drive change. It researches, plans, refers to committees, reviews, and returns reports to those committees for further review. In short, the bureaucracy simply works to keep the bureaucracy in business. It never solves anything tangible or creates anything beneficial for the stakeholders. Bureaucracy differs from hierarchy—hierarchy exists to organize and make decisions; bureaucracy exists, in theory, to carry out those decisions. In practice, it often becomes a hindrance to progress.

Bureaucracy might be the ultimate demonstration of stare decisis, the first among the status quo enemies that disruptive leaders work against.

Living in the Past

Leaders who live in the past can become so wedded to maintaining the status quo that they end up compromising the future success of their organization. They long for the "good old days," which, if you look carefully, were not always that good. Some organizations bask in nostalgia, which causes them to decline until the brink of self-destruction forces them to realize their mistakes and work to save themselves. Others are so slow to see the "writing on the wall" that they reach the point of no return. Kodak is an example of the former. When digital cameras started to become popular, Kodak kept making films until it ceased to be the world's leader in consumer photography. Blockbuster is an example of the latter. The company kept renting videotapes until there were no VCRs left.

The Herd Mentality

According to a 1927 song, "Fifty million Frenchmen can't be wrong."[32]

In reality, all those Frenchmen, plus billions of others in every country, have been and continue to be wrong about a great many things. For those who lived through the 1970s in America, I remind you of the millions of mullets barbers cut or millions of polyester leisure suits sold by clothing stores. (For younger generations, a quick Google search will boggle your mind.)

"Everybody's doing it" is a terrible reason—an excuse, I think—for doing anything. Nevertheless, there can be tremendous peer pressure to conform. Even in our current times, when branding and image are vitally important to so many products, some people buckle under peer pressure and let others take those first giant steps. An old sage once humorously suggested that "'Everybody's doing it' is *prima fascia* evidence that it's a bad idea."

Risk Aversion

Almost all people are naturally afraid of taking risks—it's part of the human survival instinct. People can also be so afraid of missing out on current opportunities that they refuse to take the risks that could bring future opportunities. Either attitude can put the entire business at risk. Because they do not look for opportunities in the marketplace, their existing products and services can become outdated. If the leadership is risk averse, the company sticks to the tried and true, whatever that might be. By refusing to buy into, sometimes even refusing to discuss, people's innovative ideas, the organization provides products or services that fewer and fewer people want to buy. It's another comfort zone problem.

---

[32] From the musical comedy *Fifty Million Frenchman*, book by Herbert Fields; music and lyrics by Cole Porter, 1929.

Strategies to Challenge the Status Quo

Disruptive leaders prioritize benefits to the organization, the common good, its followers, and all the stakeholders they represent. Nowadays, obtaining those benefits may demand taking a position or promoting policies that are not popular.

I believe that leaders need to be prepared to be unpopular because when you are a change agent, you are ahead of the group. Leading the way can cause others to say, "Hey, what is this person talking about? What is this person trying to get us to do?" They may not agree with it in its unproven form because they are stuck in their comfort zones. The process of disrupting the comfort zone is cyclic:

1. Some people will be shocked and dismissive at first, believing, "We don't need it. We don't want it."
2. They might then become actively opposed, saying, "This is just insane. We do not understand it. Nobody believes it can be done."
3. Eventually, most become a bit indifferent but start using it. "Fine. Whatever. I'll do it if it gets you to leave me alone."
4. Once it proves itself, they start liking it: "Hey, this really is easier."
5. Finally, this phase may take years, but they come to love it. "Don't you even think about taking it away!"

Many organizations have been created and transformed through this cycle. Some have repeated it time and again as they reinvent themselves to meet a new reality.

In the businesses I created, we went through all these phases, from dismissive to indispensable. During the first three stages, leaders need courageous resilience to keep at it through all the grief because you, the leader, think differently. It's easy to say but not easy to do. It can wear you down mentally and emotionally, but that is what leadership is about. Following are some strategies to disrupt the status quo:

Create a Bold Vision

> *If you don't know where you're going,*
> *you'll probably end up somewhere else.*
>
> *–David Campbell[33]*

To disrupt the status quo and bring about meaningful change, it's essential to create and foster a disruptive vision. This serves as a guiding light that helps leaders redefine what is achievable and inspires others to join its pursuit.

To create a vision, The leadership must first look at the present to see what problems exist. Then they must look into the future to see what they want the world to be like and how the present problems prevent that wonderful new world from happening. This forward-thinking approach is crucial as it allows them to identify the gaps between the present and future and formulate strategies to bridge those gaps.

It's important to note that a disruptive vision is not about making grandiose or misleading promises. The new vision must be grounded in practicality and feasibility. This means leaders should focus on crafting tangible dreams–dreams that possess the potential to bring about real change. For instance, instead of saying, "We're going to feed the world," leaders should say, "We're going to develop new agricultural methods that increase yields and reduce the effort needed to feed the world." This shift in focus acknowledges the fact that "we," whoever we are, are not the solution to the problem. We can be part of it, but others will have to do their part as well.

In addition, a compelling vision serves as a call to action for others to join the movement. It evokes emotions, ignites passion, and creates a sense of urgency. The vision must resonate with individuals on a personal level, so it motivates

---

[33] David Campbell, *If You Don't Know Where You're Going, You'll Probably End Up Somewhere Else*. Chicago: Thomas Moore Association, 1990.

them to be part of the change and contribute their unique skills and talents.

Once the vision is established, it becomes the driving force behind the strategy. It acts as the north star that guides the organization's decisions, initiatives, and actions. The vision compels leaders to ask themselves, "This is where we're going; how do we get there?" This question acts as a catalyst for innovation and fosters strategic thinking so leaders can develop a roadmap that leads to the desired future.

To create a disruptive vision, leaders must engage all relevant stakeholders. By involving diverse perspectives and encouraging collaboration, the vision becomes more inclusive and representative of collective aspirations. This ensures that individuals feel a sense of ownership and commitment and increases the likelihood of success.

So, to disrupt the status quo and drive meaningful change, leaders must cultivate a clear and compelling vision. It should be practical and feasible to inspire individuals to join the cause. By embracing creation with stakeholders, leaders harness the collective wisdom and perspectives necessary to build a vision that paves the way for a better future.

Enlist Key Stakeholders Support

There are three types of people in the world—those who make things happen, those who watch things happen, and those who wonder what happened.

—An old adage

Bringing disruptive vision to life involves actively engaging the right stakeholders and embracing necessary changes in our approach. These stakeholders—board directors, executives, investors, partners, employees, and customers–have the power to shape the trajectory and outcomes of a venture. Understanding their mindsets and the prevailing culture, and identifying potential gaps are vital to a leader. Motivating these individuals plays a crucial role in achieving our goals. Each stakeholder brings a perspective and resources that might significantly contribute to success or failure. E-level people provide financial resources, strategic guidance, and industry connections. The rank-and-file employees contribute creativity, technical expertise, and a commitment to offering a quality product. Stakeholders' deep understanding of the market and industry trends offers valuable insights.

Engaging in meaningful dialogue with key stakeholders before acting builds trust and ensures alignment. Based on my experience, I know that stakeholders who genuinely embody my venture's vision and mission are more likely to invest time, resources, and support. Their enthusiasm creates a positive and collaborative environment, fostering innovation. I go out of my way to invest significant time in building these relationships that serve as a valuable source of support and encouragement. Conversely, enlisting the wrong stakeholders can hinder progress and create a toxic work environment, no matter what their title is. Lack of support or alignment can impede decision-making processes. Stakeholders without relevant expertise limit the potential for success. Therefore, enlisting the right stakeholders with knowledge, experience, and support is critical. Their diverse perspectives, resources, and networks amplify our chances of success. Working collaboratively with stakeholders to change the status quo is crucial in achieving a disruptive outcome.

Attract the Right People to Foster Critical Thinking

To encourage critical thinking and challenge the status quo, it's crucial to bring in the right people with the right skills. Talent is the most vital resource in any endeavor. Having a great vision and understanding of how to bring about necessary change means nothing unless there are individuals who can execute these ideas effectively. Therefore, it's important to embrace diversity in all its forms, as this offers a wide range of perspectives and experiences. Including everyone and ensuring every voice is heard in decision-making processes is essential.

Leaders alone cannot drive the change required to challenge the status quo. It's necessary to motivate the entire team so that they, in turn, can motivate others. This requires attracting talented individuals, investing in developing existing team members, and providing growth opportunities for all. I believe it's vital to hire people who are better than myself in different areas of expertise—smarter, more experienced, more skilled, more articulate, or possess other skills in which they excel. Instead of being limited by our individual skills, seek out individuals who complement our strengths and bring new perspectives. We at GHD Digital couldn't have become leaders in our industry without this approach.

It's important not to always rely on the opinions of the HiPPO (highest paid person's opinion). While seniority in an organization may indicate experience and knowledge, it should not automatically mean their opinion carries the most weight. As leaders, the more senior we become, the more necessary it is to have a diverse team around us. Our position in the hierarchy should not be equated to practical knowledge. The higher we rise, the more time we've probably spent away from "the trenches" and the greater our need for the practical knowledge of those currently doing the work.

We can learn valuable lessons from individuals at middle or junior levels, particularly those who have direct engagement with clients. Leaders need to recognize that learning can come from a wide range of people and should not be limited to traditional ways of thinking dictated by hierarchical structures.

Challenging the status quo requires bringing in the right people with the right skills. By prioritizing talent and skills, we encourage critical thinking and open ourselves to new perspectives that ultimately drive positive change.

Provide Data-Driven Insights and New Perspectives

Data-driven insights and new perspectives are essential for challenging and changing the status quo. By leveraging data, we can move beyond assumptions and biases with objective insights into existing systems and processes. Insights provide a solid foundation for identifying areas of improvement and potential bottlenecks.

Further, embracing new perspectives allows us to challenge long-standing norms and approaches. It enables us to question established practices and seek alternatives. By listening to diverse perspectives, industries, and disciplines, we can tap into a wealth of ideas and fresh thinking that can revolutionize the current status quo.

In combination, data-driven insights and new perspectives provide the necessary evidence and innovative thinking that drive meaningful change to the status quo. They allow us to challenge established paradigms, identify gaps, and implement transformative strategies that can lead to improved outcomes and growth.

Find White Spaces

White spaces are key areas where you can create a niche by providing unique products and services to meet the unique needs of clients. If no one else is providing a service (or just a few small operations are), you have an opportunity if you can provide those services.

> *Red oceans are all the industries in existence today—the known market space. In red oceans, industry boundaries are defined and accepted, and the competitive rules of the game are known. Blue oceans, in contrast, denote all the industries not in existence today—the unknown market space, untainted by competition. In blue oceans, demand is created rather than fought over. There is ample opportunity for growth that is both profitable and rapid.*
>
> —Chan Kim and Renée Mauborgne[34]

Red oceans are fiercely competitive markets where everyone is fighting for the same customers and limited profits. Blue oceans, on the other hand, represent untapped opportunities, where companies can create new markets and enjoy high profitability. In between the two oceans are white spaces.

White spaces are areas where you can think differently to create your own niche and alter the status quo. It's about finding a unique way to stand out from the crowd to gain a competitive advantage. Take Porsche, for example. It established itself as a leader in the automobile industry by offering an unparalleled driving experience. People do not just buy a Porsche for transportation; they buy it for the thrill and excitement of feeling like a professional race car driver. By focusing on this unique product experience, Porsche carved out a white space for the organization and commanded a premium in the marketplace.

Implementing a white-space strategy requires experimentation, testing, and scaling up. Look at how successful companies like Uber, Facebook, and Amazon changed the status quo. They identified unmet needs and developed innovative solutions to address them. Uber seamlessly connected individuals with vehicles, ushering in a remarkable and accessible alternative to conventional taxi services. Facebook, on

---

[34] W. Chan Kim and Renée Mauborgne, *Blue Ocean Strategy, Expanded Edition: How to Create Uncontested Market Space and Make the Competition Irrelevant*. Boston: Harvard Business Review Press, 2015 (expanded edition).

the other hand, ingeniously established a platform for direct engagement and communication among people. And let us not forget the groundbreaking impact of Amazon, which completely transformed the landscape of online shopping and expedited delivery services. Do not be intimidated by the complexity or uncertainty of white spaces. Embrace them as opportunities to bring something new and valuable to the world and change the status quo. With creativity, resources, and courage, you can make it work and find success where others have yet dared to venture.

Understand the Power of Technology

Improvements in technology have driven change in human culture since humans first realized they could cultivate grain and herd beasts instead of hunting and gathering in the wild. In the twenty-first century, however, digital technology was the real disruptive feature of the times.

Today, technology is fundamentally changing the way people work and live. AI will be the next major disruptor of the status quo. The ability to leverage existing technology and blend new technologies into the status quo will blow *stare decisis* right off the planet. It's already changing the way people do business, how business models operate, and perhaps even the way people think. Digital technology, in my view, must be taken into account in any disruptive strategy.

Muster Courage and Be Brave

Build a better mousetrap, and the world will beat a path to your door.

–Old Proverb

If that is still true, beware, because some of that beating will be on the door, not the path! And the beaters will not be there to give you money. Call it courage or, bravery or valor, and it boils down to the same idea:

> *Never give in. Never give in. Never, never, never—in nothing, great or small, large or petty—never give in, except to convictions of honor and good sense. Never yield to force. Never yield to the apparently overwhelming might of the enemy.*
>
> *—Sir Winston Leonard Spencer Churchill*[35]

Resilience in the face of opposition is an essential quality that disruptive leaders possess. And criticism is inevitable when you dare to challenge the status quo. People may judge and dismiss you as a troublemaker because you disrupt their comfort zones. Others, threatened by your vision, may attack to protect their power.

Leadership, however, is not just about being a good manager; it's about guiding and inspiring others. These demands taking a stand and inviting criticism that needs the courage to withstand it. True leadership requires perseverance until the very end. This often involves personal sacrifice and even enduring pain. Consider the countless entrepreneurs who built colossal technology empires from humble beginnings, living on the edge of poverty and operating from garages. They refused to give up and ultimately achieved remarkable success.

While talent, resourcefulness, and vision are valuable, the ability to persist against formidable odds is often the differentiating factor between an upward trajectory or a disastrous downfall. Many leaders have to be willing to relinquish everything and rebuild from scratch as they embark on disruptive ventures, even after having lost it all. Courage at such a level is a rare commodity, as the fear of failure weighs heavily on individuals and impacts their families and others.

---

[35] Sir Winston Leonard Spencer Churchill, KG, OM, CH, TD, FRS, PC, "Never Give In," speech at Harrow School, 29 October 1941. *NationalChurchillMuseum.org*. Fulton, Missouri: America's National Churchill Museum. https://www.nationalchurchillmuseum.org/never-give-in-never-never-never.html, 2023, accessed 28 August, 2023.

Bravery is often discussed yet seldom genuinely displayed. A Gallup study indicated that managers willing to challenge the status quo are vastly outnumbered by those who comply. They found that just three out of one hundred dared to challenge. Most individuals prefer not to upset the established order; these are not true leaders. Leadership is a set of attitudes and actions that propel and empower one to make a meaningful difference. A true leader must possess the resilience to remain steadfast in the face of opposition. It's not easy; nothing worth having ever is, but only disruptive leaders will ever feel the fulfillment of making a difference because they understand the timeless words of Don Quixote de La Mancha:

To dream the impossible dream
To fight the unbeatable foe,
To bear with unbearable sorrow
To run where the brave dare not go.
To right the unrightable wrong
To love pure and chaste from afar,
To try when your arms are too weary
To reach the unreachable star.
This is my quest to follow that star
No matter how hopeless, no matter how far
To fight for the right without question or pause
To be willing to march into Hell for a Heavenly cause.
And I know, if I'll only be true
To this glorious quest,
That my heart will lie peaceful and calm
When I'm laid to my rest.
And the world will be better for this,
That one man, scorned and covered with scars
Still strove with his last ounce of courage
To reach the unreachable star.[36]

---

[36] "The Impossible Dream" ("The Quest"), music by Mitch Leigh, lyrics by Joe Darion, from the original Broadway cast album of *Man of La Mancha*, 1965.

Unlock New Value by Disrupting the Status Quo

To change the status quo and create new value, visionary leaders scrutinize the desires and challenges faced by their clients, the broader industry, the earth, and myriad other spheres of inquiry. The complex problems that intersect with multiple fields demand our attention. In addition, by inspecting existing technology, processes, products, and services, we uncover opportunities to create new value. The age-old question arises, "How can we deliver our current offerings more affordably, rapidly, and flexibly?"

History bears witness to the economic principle of economies of scale. Did you know that print-on-demand books were a mere notion tucked away within the pages of a science fiction magazine less than six decades ago? However, the advent of home computers and desktop printers brought this dream closer to reality, although its economic feasibility remained uncertain. Subsequently, starting with custom apparel and merchandise, books gradually became available in one-off copies rather than in bulk orders of hundreds or thousands. With the maturity of desktop publishing software, self-publishing transformed from science fiction to common technology. Today, a thriving print-on-demand industry exists, driven by numerous companies vying for your business—all because someone dared to ask, "Why not?" and unlocked the extraordinary value concealed within this concept.

Striking a balance between practical experience and new ideas is a crucial task for disruptive leaders. Disruptive leaders actively listen, embrace innovation, and harmonize past knowledge with future aspirations. They encourage and cultivate a climate of experimentation where risk-taking is respected. They embrace failure as a chance for growth, nurturing a mindset of continuous improvement. They seek feedback consistently to enhance performance while avoiding excessive self-criticism. They foster a culture of collaboration rather than one of blame to ensure that individuals take ownership and receive credit for their achievements.

Your mission, should you decide to accept it, is to disrupt the world for the benefit of others—at least, your small corner of it.

CHAPTER 7
Mental Resilience: Conquering Complacency and Fragility

In the ever-evolving, complex, post-COVID volatile and uncertain environment, disruptive leaders find themselves at the forefront of navigating uncharted territories. As world dynamics shift due to extraordinary and unpredictable global challenges, addressing mental fragility and complacency becomes crucial.

Disruptive leaders—known for their audacious vision and groundbreaking strategies—must now acknowledge that their success depends not only on external forces but also on their internal fortitude and resilience. The turbulent nature of the current landscape demands that leaders understand their own mental state and also be sensitive to the well-being of team members. They must be aware of the psychological toll that prolonged uncertainty and rapid change can have on individuals and organizations. Mental fragility, which includes vulnerability to stress, anxiety, and burnout, has become a common issue in this new reality. The relentless pace of change, decision-making with limited data, the pressure to innovate and adapt, and the responsibility of navigating uncharted territory are taking a toll on leaders' well-being.

Mental fragility for leaders in this context refers to a vulnerability that arises when facing the weight of multiple personal and professional challenges. If left unaddressed, this can impair decision-making, hinder innovation, and dull a leader's vision. It is crucial that disruptive leaders confront their vulnerabilities, foster self-reflection, and safeguard their emotional well-being to combat adversity with clarity and determination.

Complacency is equally dangerous in this environment. Leaders who fail to adapt risk torpor if they cannot keep up with how the world rapidly changes. Complacency can stem from a fear of the unknown or the overwhelming weight of multifaceted challenges. To combat this, leaders must actively cultivate a growth mindset and embrace continuous learning and personal development. By nurturing mental flexibility and adaptability, they can sidestep complacency and thrive amidst uncertainty.

Addressing mental fragility and complacency extends beyond the individual. It impacts the entire organization. A team is only as strong as its leader.

Navigating the Challenges of Mental Complacency

A leader who confines his role to his people's experience dooms himself to stagnation; a leader who outstrips his people's experience runs the risk of not being understood.

–Henry Kissinger[37]

What Is Mental Complacency?

I define mental complacency in the business world as a state of limited or stagnant thinking that inhibits growth, innovation, and adaptability within an organization. It occurs when individuals or teams become complacent, resistant to change, or unwilling to try new ideas or approaches.

In a rapidly changing business environment, mental complacency can cause missed opportunities, lack of creativity, and reduced competitiveness. It hampers the ability to identify and capitalize on emerging trends, technologies, and market demands.

---

[37] Henry Kissinger, *Diplomacy*. New York City: Simon & Schuster, 1994.

Reasons for Mental Complacency

Some key reasons for mental complacency can include the following:

- **Fear of Failure**. People may resist implementing new strategies or initiatives because they are afraid of the potential negative outcomes or repercussions. For example, a manager may be hesitant to propose a new marketing campaign for fear that if it fails to generate the projected results, his or her performance reports and bonuses may be negatively impacted.
- **Lack of Continuous Learning**. Employees who do not actively seek out new knowledge and skills can become stagnant in their thinking because they rely on outdated methods or information.
- **Resistance to Change**. When individuals or teams resist change and cling to familiar routines and processes, it can hinder progress and innovation within an organization. For example, an employee might resist using the new project management software because they prefer the traditional manual approach. This will most probably impact their efficiency in a very negative way.
- **Hierarchical or Bureaucratic Structures**. Organizations with rigid hierarchical structures or bureaucratic procedures can discourage new ideas and input from lower-level employees, which can create mental complacency. For instance, in a top-down authoritarian organization, employees may feel discouraged from sharing their ideas or suggestions.
- **Lack of Feedback and Constructive Criticism**. Without honest feedback and constructive criticism, employees may remain unaware of their blind spots or areas for improvement, which can cause a stagnant mindset.
- **Failure to Embrace Diversity and Inclusion**. A lack of diversity in teams and an unwillingness to value different perspectives can limit creative thinking and innovation, resulting in mental complacency. For instance, if a company only hires individuals from similar backgrounds and experiences, it misses out on the benefits of diverse thinking and fresh ideas.

- **Burnout and Overwhelm.** High levels of stress and overwhelming workloads can lead to mental exhaustion and a narrowed focus on day-to-day tasks, impeding broader thinking.
- **Resting on Past Laurels.** Resting on past achievements without seeking new challenges or goals can breed a sense of complacency and hinder intellectual growth. For instance, a company that has experienced a period of rapid growth may become complacent and fail to explore new markets or innovative products.
- **Lack of Encouragement to Innovate.** When organizations do not foster a culture that encourages and rewards innovation, employees may feel discouraged from thinking outside the box and generating new ideas. For example, if managers consistently dismiss or ignore employee suggestions for improvement, employees will simply stop suggesting innovations.
- **Lack of Accountability.** Mistakes happen, we are human. Some mistakes can be dismissed, but others demand a penalty be paid, and failing to demand that payment encourages bad behavior. For example, if an employee is consistently late to work or takes long lunch breaks, other employees will feel empowered to be lazy about their work habits.

These factors contribute to mental complacency, individual or collective, which stifles progress and limits people's ability to adapt and thrive in our rapidly changing business landscape. Disruptive leaders must remain vigilant toward these factors and proactively work to overcome mental complacency. Fostering a culture of continuous learning and growth is vital to maintain team or corporate growth.

Strategies to Challenge Mental Complacency
Learn to Unlearn and Upskill Yourself

The speed at which knowledge becomes outdated is astonishing. Beliefs held twenty, fifteen, or even ten years ago have been disproven in many cases. This is particularly evident in business management, where principles from previous generations no longer hold true. In today's dynamic world, technology, education, and societal changes require an evolution in management approaches. Genuine leadership now supersedes traditional management ideologies, prompting a need to unlearn and adapt.

Groundbreaking discoveries are constantly made in different fields, such as medicine, technology, science, politics, and the arts. So it's illogical to assume that leadership and inspiration should remain rooted in methods from one hundred or even fifty years ago. Holding onto outdated knowledge and paradigms hinders progress. Just as we replace obsolete equipment, our approaches to personal interactions must also be replaced with advanced methods.

Reflecting on my own skill set, I constantly assess the value I bring to my stakeholders. Technical upskilling was crucial to maintaining competence early in my career. However, the importance of soft skills grew as I transitioned into management and leadership roles, so I intentionally developed those areas. Running my own businesses required nurturing creative and entrepreneurial skills. Additionally, serving as a spokesperson for industry groups demanded comprehensive industry knowledge to effectively communicate with media outlets and politicians.

These are just a few of the skills I had to acquire throughout my career. Professional growth necessitates continuous learning, with the realization that upskilling oneself to become a better leader is essential. I constantly expand my knowledge by consuming numerous books each month to explore new areas. This relentless pursuit of self-improvement is an integral part of my journey.

It's important to note that the personal and professional aspects of our lives require ongoing learning. As individuals, coworkers, leaders, parents, children, neighbors, and friends, we must strive for improvement in our relationships. The learning journey is boundless and ever-present.

Self-assessment and Awareness

Self-assessment and awareness are vital tools for business leaders to challenge mental complacency and drive innovation. By continuously evaluating their own abilities, biases, and limitations, leaders can identify areas for growth and development. Here are two examples of how to apply self-assessment and awareness:

- **Reflecting on Technological Advancements.** Digital professional services leaders should ask themselves questions such as, "Am I up to date with the latest digital tools and platforms? Are there any knowledge gaps that I need to address? How can I ensure my team is continuously learning to stay ahead?"
- **Recognizing Leadership Strengths and Weaknesses.** Effective leaders must assess their leadership style and be aware of their strengths and weaknesses. This self-awareness enables them to leverage their strengths for the benefit of their team and to seek assistance or development in areas where they may be lacking. Through self-reflection and feedback from peers and subordinates, leaders can proactively address any issues and improve their leadership skills.

Seek the Gift of Feedback

The gift of feedback is a powerful approach to combat mental complacency for leaders. By actively seeking input from others and seeing it as a blessing, they can gain valuable insights, challenge their assumptions, and propel personal and professional growth.

I recognize the gift of critique in driving innovation and overcoming mental complacency. I regularly seek feedback from my team, clients, and industry experts to gain a holistic perspective on my leadership style and business direction and identify areas for improvement. Recently, during a strategic planning meeting, I actively invited my team members to share their thoughts on the business's successes and challenges. My team includes more than just those who just report to me;

it also includes my peers and leaders to whom I report. I call these sessions "Radical candor with respect" sessions.

By openly listening to my team's feedback, I gain new insights into potential areas of complacency within our company's processes. I encourage a culture of psychological safety where everyone feels comfortable expressing their ideas and suggestions. This feedback allows me to reassess our existing strategies, implement necessary changes, and infuse fresh perspectives to effectively tackle business challenges. Indeed, within the walls of my home, my beloved daughter Sreya and wife, Paddy, graciously offer me their candid feedback, to which I strive to respond in kind, albeit not always with perfect success.

Feedback allows me to continue to convert mental complacency into a catalyst for growth and innovation. My openness to feedback not only challenges my own thinking but empowers my team to contribute their ideas freely, which leads to enhanced creativity, collaboration, and business success.

Someone once asked a wise man, "What's the difference between *critique* and *criticism*?"

That old sage responded, "In *criticism*, you say, 'This is what I don't like about you.' In *critique*, you say, 'This is what I like about what you're doing, and this is how I think you can do it better.'"

Sounded like as good a definition as I'll ever hear.

Ignite Meaningful Conversations

Creating positive change by constructively challenging the status quo necessitates engaging in meaningful conversations. Here are the strategies I employ in a professional services business:

- **I focus** on setting the stage for open dialogue and honesty. I foster a nonjudgmental environment where team members and stakeholders feel secure giving honest feedback as well as their thoughts and ideas. By creating a safe space, I encourage trust and vulnerability. Seeking feedback from my employees, peers, board members, and executives ensures a comprehensive understanding of potential blind spots.
- **I believe** in establishing bold goals that push individual capabilities. Together with my team members, I co-create ambitious targets, emphasizing their significance while detaching them from a personal appraisal. Acknowledging challenges promotes collaboration and provides valuable learning opportunities for knowledge expansion.
- **I celebrate** both small and significant team successes, nurturing a culture of achievement. Alongside celebration, maintaining accountability is crucial to keep everyone focused on meeting set goals.
- **I encourage** a growth mindset by inspiring ambitious goals, coupled with ample learning opportunities. I genuinely appreciate individuals' dedication and approach discussions with respect and care. This fosters productive conversations that lead to personal growth and development.

By fostering an environment of constructive dialogue, setting ambitious goals, and respecting efforts, we create a culture that drives out mental complacency. With a shared commitment to ongoing growth and innovation, both individuals and the organization thrive in an environment of continuous improvement.

Embrace Diversity and Inclusion with Open Arms

Diversity and inclusion are essential not only for fostering a fair and equitable workplace but also for addressing individual and organizational mental complacency. True diversity goes beyond a mere "tick in the box" approach. It encompasses a variety of backgrounds, experiences, perspectives, and ways of thinking. This is true diversity of thought that has the potential to challenge existing norms, break down silos, and ignite innovative thinking.

By valuing diversity and inclusion, an organization creates a platform where people from all backgrounds feel empowered to share their unique insights and experiences. A diverse range of perspectives acts as a catalyst for shaking up stagnant mentalities. By welcoming fresh ideas and alternative viewpoints, organizations evolve from traditional thinking and avoid the pitfalls of groupthink that hinder growth and innovation.

Further, encouraging an inclusive culture ensures that all voices are heard and valued. This allows individuals to feel psychologically safe and lets them be more authentic at work. People are more likely to challenge prevailing ideas, engage in constructive debates, and provide valuable feedback in this environment. It's through honest and open exchanges that mental complacency can be disrupted, creating a space that thrives on continuous learning, adaptation, and growth.

GHD Digital embraced diversity and inclusion as a foundational principle at its inception in 2018. From day one, we ensured that our team comprised individuals from diverse backgrounds, including a 50 percent representation of women, individuals of different races, and varying age groups. As one of the first few individuals of Indian origin to hold senior positions in Australia, such as CIO in the Queensland Government, KPMG partner in Australia, ACS chairman, and as founding president of GHD Digital, I've had the rare privilege and honor of witnessing the power of diversity and inclusion firsthand. Drawing from experiences, I knew that to create a global business like GHD Digital, we needed a diverse leadership team that could think creatively and solve problems in innovative ways. Today, we take pride in the fact that two out of our four businesses are led by exceptionally talented women, and, until recently, it was three out of four.

We attribute our continued success to the power of diversity and inclusion, as it fuels our ability to think differently, drive innovation, and foster a culture of collaboration. We believe that when individuals from diverse backgrounds come together, they not only bring unique perspectives but also create an environment that celebrates and embraces the strengths of every individual. We are committed to maintaining and strengthening our diversity and inclusion priorities as we continue to make a positive impact.

Stirring the Pot

I love stirring the pot. It challenges teams. Not everybody loves me stirring the pot, especially the happily complacent, but I still stir that pot, and I do it with a very large spoon. It creates a positive change by constructively challenging the limiting beliefs and helps conquer complacency.

First, I set the stage:

- I encourage people to be honest and forthright and have frequent conversations.
- I guarantee them a safe environment in which they can share their thoughts and ideas without fear of judgment or appraisal.
- Sometimes, I share my concerns, vulnerabilities, and feelings with them.
- I am open to saying, "I'm worried about this. I don't know the right answer."

All this encourages people to speak up so they overcome their mental barriers. Sometimes it can be confronting, but when people know it's for their benefit and the collective good, they'll speak up.

Second, I set bold goals that demand people stretch:

- I will explain my bold goals—why we are not setting business-as-usual goals and what those goals intend to accomplish.

- I remind them that whether they achieve it or not, it's not going to make any difference in how I feel about them.
- I recognize that they will inevitably face challenges and setbacks along the way, which encourages them to collaborate with other team members to do better or more than they could on their own.
- I provide opportunities for them to expand their knowledge so they can conquer obstacles, which makes them far less susceptible to mental complacency.
- We celebrate team successes, small and large, regularly.
- Through it all, I insist they come to work and strive to meet those goals. I hold them accountable because if they do not feel like they are accountable for their actions, it's a nonstarter. They are not motivated to work.

All the great ideas in the world—the ones that may bring marvelous, positive changes—are worthless if people do not feel a fire lighting up inside them. The bold goals should inspire; the accountability process should keep them on track; the challenges should keep them humble; and the learning opportunities should keep their minds at peak efficiency. When you move forward, it naturally draws others forward, and their motion naturally draws you forward. It becomes a self-sustaining cycle of achievement.

Of course, we find situations where initiatives go awry. A team might expend huge amounts of resources—time, effort, money—but still find people attached to their old ways because they cannot challenge their mental complacency. At such times, despite our best efforts, they may not recognize that their initiative is not really going the way it needs to go.

This is where real disruptive leadership moments are born. You, the team leader, sometimes must constructively challenge team members to pivot despite the fact that it makes them uncomfortable. Fortunately, when a team gets deeply into implementation, a thorough, constructive dialogue that identifies issues and proposes solutions can get people to make that pivot and get back on track for success.

Notice that I specifically do not say, "Get people to change." You cannot. People only change when they want to; it cannot be forced on them. When I encourage people to pivot, I'm showing them new possibilities, which, I hope, will attract them so much that *they want to change* the way they do things to achieve those possibilities.

My simple view of the world is positive. I believe people are trying to do their best nine times out of ten. Occasionally, lazy people who just want to get by slip into any system, but these people usually situate themselves in jobs that can be done robotically. They aren't comfortable in companies with disruptive leaders because they do not want to change. They find themselves a groove and stay in it. These are, I think, a small minority of people.

Most people want to better themselves, and when people feel a need to change, you just need to engage them with empathy, a little love, a bit of genuine care, and never be skeptical about their intentions in relation to what you've asked them to do. You can rarely help them move forward, help them pivot, embrace change, or make them more accountable if you come at them from a "Hey, I'm the boss. You tell me what you're doing, and I'll decide whether you're doing a good job or not" perspective. If, instead, you come to them with a "Hey, you're already doing a great job, and I see you trying your best. Now, if you were to pivot your perspective just a little bit this way, I'm confident you'll be an even greater success, as will the whole team."—with that as a lead-in, they will be ready to have a discussion.

Always respect the good efforts—effective or not so effective—of your people. Assume they are doing their best, giving it their best shot. Even when they are not moving as fast as we would like or expect, when you give them the respect they deserve as people and engage with them in a professional manner, you can spark a desire in them to change themselves and create the best success they can.

There is not one among us—me as certainly as anyone else—that cannot do better. Stirring the pot in the right way makes people *want* to do better, and that is the surest way I know to drive out mental complacency.

Conquer Mental Fragility

> *You don't have to control your thoughts.*
> *You just have to stop letting them control you.*
>
> —Dan Millman[38]

COVID-19 significantly increased mental fragility in several ways. The rapid spread, severity, and economic impact of the virus generated uncertainty and fear, which increased levels of stress, anxiety, and depression. Social isolation and loneliness worsened because of lockdowns, quarantines, and social distancing measures, all of which negatively impacted mental well-being. Financial pressures from job losses, pay cuts, and business closures created more anxiety, stress, and mental health difficulties. Increased work demands and burnout, whether from remote work or heavier workloads, have reduced mental resilience. Additionally, concerns about health and grief resulting from the threat of infection or the loss of loved ones amplified psychological distress. Limited access to mental health support further exacerbated the situation. As such, it's crucial to prioritize mental health support and implement resilience-building strategies.

The Impact of Mental Fragility

Again, a state of vulnerability or susceptibility to stress, anxiety, and depression are signs of mental fragility. In the context of leadership, resilience in dynamic business and global environments, as well as mental fragility, can hinder an individual's ability to cope with the demands and pressures

---

[38] Dan Millman, *You Don't Have to Control Your Thoughts. You Just Have to Stop Letting Them Control You*. (Independently published), 2023.

of their leadership role. Several factors contribute to mental fragility in such environments:

- **Uncertainty and Complexity.** Dynamic, rapidly changing business and global environments often present leaders with unpredictable and complex situations. Constantly facing uncertainty can create a sense of mental or emotional drowning.
- **High Expectations and Pressure.** Leaders are expected to perform at a high level and make critical decisions under pressure. The relentless pursuit of success and the fear of failure can contribute to mental exhaustion.
- **Work-Life Balance.** Maintaining a healthy work-life balance is crucial for mental well-being. However, in dynamic environments, leaders often face long working hours, travel demands, and an "always-on" culture that can lead to burnout.
- **Isolation and Lack of Social Support.** With increased responsibilities, leaders may experience feelings of isolation and pressure to maintain a strong front. The lack of a supportive network or the inability to share concerns openly can contribute to depression and other mental issues.
- **Rapid Change.** Dynamic environments require leaders to be adaptable and embrace change. However, constantly adjusting to new circumstances can cause stress and a feeling of being mentally drained—as if one is a transmission whose gears have been stripped.

Strategies to Deal with Mental Fragility

Do not let the setbacks crush you. Bounce back by recognizing them as a growth opportunity.

Dealing with mental fragility requires implementing strategies to enhance resilience and promote well-being. Here are a few effective strategies to consider:

Winning in Your mind

"The thought precedes the action" is an ancient idea. Winning in your mind before you win in life gives leaders the power to transform their and others' lives. An objective so clear that you can see it before it happens plays a significant role in overcoming challenges, achieving goals, and developing resilience. By adopting this "I've already won" mentality, one can replace fragility with strength and resilience.

To start, I define winning as personal growth, progress, and overcoming obstacles. It's about accepting challenges as growth opportunities despite all that life throws at me. It's easier said than done, but that is the objective, and with practice, it can become your default mental position. I understand that in the journey toward progress, it's inevitable that we encounter mistakes along the way, which provide opportunities for learning and growth. It's important to remember that we should not be overly critical of ourselves for making mistakes but embrace them as stepping stones toward our ultimate disruptive goals.

Conquering mental fragility requires cultivating a positive and resilient mindset. I actively challenge my negative thoughts and often replace them with affirmations, self-assurances, and determination to learn and grow. Visualization techniques also help me imagine the desired state and strengthen my mental fortitude. I visualize overcoming challenges and embodying the qualities of resilience.

Getting the Monkey Mind under Control

The "monkey mind" refers to the constant movement of the mind, jumping from one thought to another, usually without focus or purpose. It can lead to anxiety, stress, and a lack of mental clarity. When our minds are constantly racing and scattered, it becomes difficult to maintain resilience in the face of challenges. From a mental resilience perspective, this concept holds great significance in Eastern philosophies.

Getting my monkey mind under control is crucial for cultivating my mental resilience. Constantly fixating on potential problems and contemplating all that can go wrong can have a serious impact on one's mental well-being. It's essential to focus only on matters within your control and refrain from overthinking things outside your sphere of influence. By doing so, you can effectively preserve your mental stability and deal with mental fragility. Developing control over the monkey mind is crucial for cultivating mental resilience. By quieting this mind state, we can enhance our ability to focus and direct our energy toward productive actions. It also helps with emotional regulation, problem-solving abilities, and self-awareness.

To control the monkey mind, I've used practices such as meditation, controlled breathing, and journaling. These allow us to observe our thoughts without getting caught up in them so we can validate and control them. This, in turn, strengthens our mental resilience, enabling us to navigate challenges with grace and perseverance. (Effective use of these techniques does require consistent practice.)

Thought Replacement and Self-talk

When we think about problems, our problems grow. When we think about solutions, our solutions grow.

—Jason Selk[39]

During a recent conversation with friends, I stumbled on a new meaning for the abbreviation "BMW," which surprisingly did not refer to the well-known car company. Instead, it stood for "blaming, moaning, and whining"–traits associated with a victim mentality. This revelation made me reflect on how frequently we tend to shift blame and dwell on problems rather than seek solutions.

---

[39] Jason Selk, *10-Minute Toughness: The Mental Training Program for Winning Before the Game Begins*. New York City: McGraw Hill, 2008.

The victim mindset arises when we succumb to blaming, moaning, and whining during challenges or moments of discouragement, convinced that external circumstances hinder our progress. However, it's vital to recognize and overcome this mindset by taking personal responsibility and redirecting our thoughts toward constructive solutions.

To combat the victim mentality, I find value in thought replacement and self-talk techniques. I aspire to be solution-focused rather than dwell on negative thoughts. By determining the desired solution in a given situation, I actively focus my mind on the thoughts and steps required to achieve them. This shift in thinking significantly increases my chances of success, a principle that applies to other areas of life as well, including business and social interactions. Instead of fixating on obstacles, I choose to concentrate on the path to success and channel my energy into attaining it.

I also understand the importance of self-confidence in enhancing performance, with self-talk playing a vital role in bolstering it. So I ensure that my internal dialogue aligns with my pursuit of excellence, which is of utmost importance.

Additionally, I know that conflicting thoughts cannot coexist in our minds. This presents an exciting opportunity to swiftly replace negative thoughts with positive ones. By disciplining myself and becoming aware of how often my mind dwells on worst-case scenarios or perceived barriers, I prioritize focusing on desired outcomes in business and relationships.

Develop a Support System of Trusted Advisors

Building a good support network and relationships is essential in addressing the challenges of mental fragility. Here are some steps I have taken:

- **Identify Supportive Individuals.** Look for people in your life who are empathetic, understanding, and genuinely care about your well-being. They can be friends, family

- members, colleagues, or even professionals like therapists or support groups.
- **Communicate Your Needs**. Discuss your challenges and mental health concerns with your support network. Explain what support you require, whether it's a listening ear, advice, or assistance in seeking professional help.
- **Participate in Communities**. Join support groups or online communities where people with similar challenges come together. Being part of a group that understands your experiences can provide validation, empathy, and practical advice.
- **Foster Healthy Relationships**. Nourish the relationships that uplift you and make you feel supported. Invest time and effort in building connections based on trust, respect, and mutual understanding.
- **Set Boundaries**. Be mindful of your boundaries and communicate them effectively with your support network. It's crucial to establish limits to avoid feeling overwhelmed or stretched too thin.
- **Practice Active Listening**. Strengthen your relationships by actively listening to others, showing empathy, and providing a nonjudgmental space. Being supportive of others creates a reciprocal environment of support.
- **Prioritize Self-care**. Focus on your personal well-being by routinely engaging in activities that reduce stress, promote relaxation, and enhance self-esteem. Self-care positively impacts your ability to navigate challenges and maintain healthy relationships.

Remember, building a strong support network of empathic people takes time and effort. Be patient, open-minded, and proactive in seeking and maintaining these relationships.

Establish Routines and Structure

I found establishing routines and structure an effective strategy for dealing with mental fragility. Having structure in our daily lives provides stability and predictability, which can be calming and comforting.

- **Create Routines**. Establishing consistent daily routines can help bring a sense of order to your life. This can include setting regular wake-up and bedtimes, scheduling meals and breaks, and incorporating activities that promote relaxation and self-care. Routines provide a foundation for stability and can reduce feelings of overwhelm and unpredictability.
- **Set Achievable Goals**. Clearly defining and working toward achievable goals is another important aspect of establishing structure. Start by identifying realistic and meaningful goals that align with your values and aspirations. Break them down into smaller, actionable steps, and create a schedule to allocate time and resources for each task. This helps provide a sense of purpose, direction, and accomplishment, which can boost mental well-being.
- **Implement Boundaries**. Structure also involves setting boundaries in your personal and professional life. This means learning to say no to excessive demands, setting limits on the use of technology and social media, and establishing boundaries in relationships. Boundaries help protect your time, energy, and mental health, allowing you to maintain a healthier balance and reduce stress.

By establishing routines and structure, we organize in life. This enables me to manage my time better, reduces the possibility of becoming overwhelmed, and fosters a sense of control over my circumstances. I've said that routine can lead to mental complacency. However, humans subconsciously crave things that are familiar, so a measured, controlled routine can contribute to your overall mental resilience and help in dealing with mental fragility.

Overall, as a leader, you need to be aware of the toll that uncertainty and rapid changes have on you and those around you in this post-COVID culture. You may become mentally fragile trying to keep up with the fast pace and trying to make decisions without all the necessary data. Being under constant pressure to innovate and adapt and the responsibility of navigating new territory can negatively affect your well-being. So you need to foster your emotional well-being by confronting your vulnerabilities and taking time out for self-reflection.

If you do not adapt to the fast-moving environment, you are at risk of stagnating and succumbing to mental fragility. You may feel burdened and overwhelmed by so many challenges or a fear of the unknown. So it's important to adopt a disruptive mindset and an attitude that drives you to continuously learn and focus on self-development. Being adaptable will help you to avoid complacency and thrive in an uncertain, fast-paced world.

CHAPTER 8

What Accountability Means and Why Results Matter

Accountability breeds responsibility.
—Stephen Richards Covey[40]

Disruptive leaders' accountability transcends the confines of a business unit or their specific team. It extends to their company, their industry, their community, and even the whole world. They bear responsibility not only toward their subordinates, managers, and boards but also to their shareholders and other stakeholders. Accountability reaches beyond mere adherence to rules and regulations. It also encompasses their moral and ethical obligations. The notion of a disruptive leader's accountability is twofold:

- **Leaders must assume personal accountability**—especially those who disrupt the norm. They own their actions, decisions, and behavior and proactively manage their responsibilities, accepting the consequences of their choices. They likewise need to recognize that unforeseen circumstances can occur and take responsibility for addressing and resolving whatever results may arise. Disruptive leaders do not make excuses.
- **Leaders must maintain business accountability**. This involves evaluating how the business operates to ensure its success and alignment with the shared vision, mission, goals, and objectives established by the owners and managers. It's essential to honestly assess whether the business is operating legally while also

---

[40] Stephen R Covey, *The 7 Habits of Highly Effective People: Powerful Lessons in Personal Change*. New York City: Free Press (an imprint of Simon & Schuster), 1989.

meeting the expectations of employees, clients, suppliers, shareholders, and other stakeholders. Disruptive leaders do not sugarcoat their outcomes.

By embracing both personal and business accountability, disruptive leaders create a foundation of trust, transparency, and ethical behavior to drive organizations toward sustainable success. The key accountabilities of disruptive leaders are similar to any other business leader, but the context of their accountabilities is different and includes the following:

- **They often make larger investments** in innovation, new products, or new business models. Accounting standards can view this negatively. The finance department might write them off before there is a return on investment, even though there is potential for greater growth or margins. Accountability in this context involves effectively communicating the value of the investment to bring others on board while also being prepared to make difficult decisions if an investment is not successful.
- **They frequently venture into uncharted territory** as they disrupt the market. They require professionals with diverse experiences and mindsets who may stand out as different from the organizational norm. Unfortunately, traditionalists within the organization may not appreciate the unique perspectives these individuals bring. The challenge for disruptive leaders lies in maintaining the courage to hire the people they need to get the job done and support these professionals, even in the face of criticism.

Specific areas of focus for disruptive leaders include these:

- **Vision and Strategy**. They must create a vision that people buy into and a long-term plan to make it happen.
- **Talent Management**. They must attract, develop, and retain top talent, creating a culture that nurtures innovation and collaboration.

- **Customer Focus**. They must understand their client needs and preferences, focus on the problem they're trying to solve, and continuously evaluate market trends to meet and exceed customer expectations.
- **Innovation**. They strive for "the next great thing," not only within their organizations but also throughout existing markets and industries.
- **Financial Management**. They accept responsibility for achieving established financial results. They manage all financial aspects of their projects, including budgeting, planning, resource allocation, and they monitor performance to ensure the business remains sustainable and profitable.
- **Risk Management**. They assess and manage potential risks. They analyze the potential impact of their actions on every aspect of the organization, especially compliance with regulations. They make informed decisions based on all the available facts.
- **Stakeholder Management**. They proactively manage relationships with stakeholders. They understand and address stakeholder needs and interests while maintaining open, positive relationships.
- **Learning and Adaptability**. They learn continuously, adapting to the rapid changes in the business landscape and end-user expectations. They know the up-to-date industry standards and trends, always with an eye to "What comes next?"
- **Ethical Conduct**. They maintain high ethical standards in all business practices and demand the same of their people.

It's important to note that these responsibilities will vary depending on the specific context, the industry, and individual leadership styles.

Throughout the years, many business leaders have seriously compromised their personal ethics and business responsibilities, leading to losses of billions of dollars, thousands of jobs, and on occasion, their freedom. We have witnessed instances where investors poured millions of dollars into companies, only to have mismanagement run rampant while the board and auditors turned a blind eye. Financial reporting suffered greatly from misleading information—and disastrous results.

This grim reality necessitated tightening corporate governance regulations, such as the Sarbanes-Oxley Act, which introduced stringent standards of accountability for management and board members of publicly listed companies. At one time, a large number of my team members were involved in helping companies comply with these requirements. Although compliance proved burdensome and complex, they raised the bar for responsibility and accountability that corporate leaders—the C-suite people—must demonstrate to be recognized as truly fulfilling their duties. Investors and shareholders have an inherent right to know what happens within the companies they invest in, that their investments are not misused, and that organizations comply with all applicable rules and regulations.

Taking Responsibility for Performance and Results

Disruptive leaders measure themselves by the outcomes they achieve. At the beginning of each year, to ensure alignment and progress, our team develops a business plan that includes financial and nonfinancial KPIs (key performance indicators)—for example, customer satisfaction, branding, thought leadership, and employee retention. Developing twelve to fourteen KPIs is a measurement system that allows for a holistic evaluation of our business progress.

These KPIs assist our team in maintaining accountability for performance. Results are paramount in driving success and achieving organizational goals, and they must be held to a higher standard than other leaders. A disruptive leader is responsible for setting clear expectations, challenging the status quo, and delivering exceptional outcomes. They are accountable for driving growth, innovation, and operational excellence. For instance, a disruptive leader may implement new strategies and processes to improve efficiency, resulting in increased productivity and cost savings. Disruptive leaders can also spearhead new product development initiatives that lead to revenue growth and market expansion. In addition, they empower their teams by providing guidance and support to ensure individual and collective success.

Two common misconceptions cloud the true understanding of accountability:

- It's believed to be entirely associated with non-performance issues.
- It's viewed as a one-time event.

But here's the truth:

- Accountability for team members' performance and results is not a stick to beat people up with when things do not go to plan.
- Accountability should be an ongoing dialogue between managers and employees.

Many of us have experienced the positive effects of accountability when encouraged by senior leaders to reach our potential. Unfortunately, in some organizations, accountability tends to be unclear, rewards misused, consequences diluted or nonexistent, and the correlation between outcomes and recognition remains hazy.

When practiced appropriately, accountability inspires a culture of excellence where achievements are recognized and valued. It's a crucial enabler to bring out the best in people. Over the years, I've learned that my personal and business success relies on a balanced approach between financial results and driving change through innovation. On the one hand, if you compromise financial results, the business will not have the capacity to sustain its short-term demands. On the other hand, if the innovation agenda is compromised, the business may not have a long-term future.

Accountability doesn't only show us when our people are falling short; it also shows when they are leaping ahead.

In new ventures focused on disruptive transformation, you're creating new products and services with no track record. You're experimenting with what can disrupt the current state of affairs. In these situations, things rarely go as planned, so it's vital that disruptive leaders proactively communicate and provide stakeholders with objective information to keep their support. When things go wrong, the skeptics jump in, and investors may start doubting everything. Again, it's necessary to make full disclosure and transparently explain the reasons for deviation. I often enlist these stakeholders to address the challenges on the disruptive path and get their help in making course corrections. This gives them a personal and reputational stake in the outcome. Talk about getting people motivated to support you!

There are a few key areas that always have a huge impact on the success of disruptive leaders:

- Mutual accountability among stakeholders
- Building and empowering the right teams
- Making tough decisions
- Full accountability to stakeholders
- Managing business risks

These accountabilities determine the success of disruptive leaders and any venture they lead.

Mutual Accountability Among Stakeholders

Do what you say you'll do, and demand others do what they said they would.

It's not solely the responsibility of disruptive leaders to be held accountable to their stakeholders. Rather, it's a reciprocal duty. The board and executives must establish an environment that fosters and empowers disruptive leaders. Leadership that challenges the status quo and readies their organizations for the future cannot be cultivated and nurtured without a culture that encourages disruptive thinking.

In my view, this is one of the primary reasons why organizations stagnate for decades. They become insular, resistant to external perspectives and market changes, and consumed by their internal reality at every level. The decision-making authority of boards and executives is tightly controlled, often prioritizing compliance over competence when determining membership at these upper echelons.

While this approach may suffice during prosperous market conditions, it becomes precarious when the tides shift, and a lack of skills jeopardizes the survival of the organization.

Disruptive leadership possesses an undeniable potency, fueling transformative change and propelling organizations forward into an uncertain future. To do this, it must have the unwavering support and invaluable guidance provided by boards and executives. In a world marked by constant and rapid change, the presence of disruptive leaders becomes even more crucial in fortifying organizations against uncertainties that lie ahead.

The path of disruptive leadership is often hindered when confronted by executives resistant to change or those who prioritize strict control, sometimes for self-gain or political reasons. Faced with such challenges, disruptive leaders find themselves trapped in a dilemma—compromising their visionary ideas or risking failure altogether. Undeterred by obstacles, disruptive leaders maintain an unyielding determination. However, their success cannot be achieved in isolation. Boards and CEOs play an integral role in cultivating a culture that wholeheartedly encourages and sustains this leadership.

I've been fortunate to have the opportunity to thrive within environments like those at KPMG and GHD. Global boards and executives of these companies showcased remarkable foresight and collective wisdom by wholeheartedly supporting disruptive endeavors, thereby enabling the infusion of a diverse range of talents and skills necessary to drive innovation. I am forever indebted to the late Michael Andrew, KPMG Global Chairman, and Rob Knott, GHD's Global Chairman, for setting an exemplary standard for transformative change at the top of their companies with nearly a century of heritage and success. Their unwavering support paved the way for people like me to start disruptive ventures, infuse diverse talents and develop the skills necessary to drive innovation and build new global businesses at scale. The question often posed by leaders is, "Are we doing enough? Should we be moving faster?" resonates deeply within me.

As I reflect on the early years of establishing GHD Digital, I am filled with gratitude for the opportunity to assemble an exceptional top team of forty-five to fifty individuals who lead our six-hundred person business. Each one brought their own distinctive perspectives and extraordinary skill sets, quite different from the existing talent pool. The integration of these forward-thinking innovators with our already exceptional workforce of engineers and scientists was undoubtedly a blessing.

Collaborating closely with my esteemed GHD colleagues such as the Americas CEO, Jim Giannopoulos; Asia-Pacific CEO, Ian Fraser; Global CFOs, Phil Bradley and, later, Marc Armstrong; Global CCO Sonia Adams; and GHD Advisory President, Richard Fechner has been an absolute privilege. Together, we have nurtured dynamic teams who spearheaded transformative change across our global enterprise. This resulted in significant progress within a relatively short timeframe, surpassing what our competitors had achieved in decades, contributing to the creation of GHD Digital, recognized as the digital transformation leader in the $200B AEC industry by EFCG in January 2024.[41]

By acknowledging the indispensability of disruptive leadership, organizations effectively future-proof themselves, ensuring continued success and relevance in a rapidly changing world.

---

[41] (Unbylined), "EFCG Reports Latest Findings on Technology and Innovation Leadership in the AEC Industry," *BusinessWire.com*. San Francisco: Berkshire Hathaway, 29 January 2024. https://www.businesswire.com/news/home/20240129619968/en/EFCG-Reports-Latest-Findings-on-Technology-and-Innovation-Leadership-in-the-AEC-Industry, accessed 1 March 2024.

Building and Empowering the Right Team

Disruptive leaders understand the importance of building the right teams and empowering them. They take accountability for nurturing and developing their team members, providing opportunities for growth, mentorship, and continuous learning. Their goal is to foster a positive work environment that enables employees to reach their full potential.

In overseeing a global business, I took a careful approach to team building. While I participate in or lead the process of choosing the top twenty leaders, they then become involved in selecting the rest of the team. Building a team that delivers disruptive outcomes, where there is sometimes no precedence, is like completing a jigsaw puzzle. Conventional wisdom states that everybody is a square, and when you put all the squares together, you get a perfect picture, even if you have to scrape the edges off a few round holes in order to jam them into those square holes.

Reality is far different. That traditional approach to team building may have worked once, but not anymore. We are experiencing challenges that never existed before. So, to deal with these and to create an effective team, it's essential that leaders recognize and leverage the individuality and strengths of the diverse talent pool.

Job descriptions are a starting point. I do not simply rely on job descriptions or believe in pigeonholing individuals after a rigorous evaluation process when hiring top leaders for disruptive ventures. Instead, I focus on understanding their dreams, how they want to leave a positive impact; their personal and professional plans; and what motivates them. By aligning their passions and motivations with the business needs, we craft a role that becomes their "dream job" with clear, measurable KPIs.

Aligning the team around common goals and fostering a high-impact, disruptive environment requires constant nurturing and challenges. It's a continuous process that helps the team reach its best potential. The emphasis is on combining individual strengths and working together toward shared objectives rather than solely focusing on individual goals.

By embracing the uniqueness of each team member and strategically aligning their strengths, we create a high-performance culture that drives exceptional results.

When empowered, right teams with a shared purpose can greatly boost goal attainment and drive transformative results. A standout instance I participated in was the leadership development initiative led by Jan Sipsma, GHD's Chief People Officer. Jan coached top leaders to adopt a 'team of teams' approach, contributing to an accelerated pace of positive change across a diverse global organisation.

Empowering

Always look out for the best interests of the people you lead.

I believe in the power of empowerment, accountability, and direction to drive team effectiveness. It's essential for every team member to actively contribute and collaborate, working seamlessly together to generate momentum and set the team's direction. Collaboration may present challenges, but it's an integral part of our success.

As a leader, it's imperative to consistently support and protect those who rely on you and report to you. You must ensure their well-being and safeguard them from undue harm or negative criticism they may encounter while carrying out their responsibilities. Your unwavering commitment to "having their back" amplifies a culture of trust and fosters an environment where individuals can confidently fulfill their duties.

Diversity Matters

For me, the right team is a diverse team. Diversity is not limited to just representatives of various backgrounds in the team; it's "diversity of thought" based on a variety of experiences and backgrounds. The principle of diversity of thought has enabled us to create extraordinary teams that could achieve unthinkable breakthroughs and drive groundbreaking innovation. Again, the right team that is competent enough to drive financial results and innovative outcomes is the holy grail—that's what we've accomplished in the last few years.

I believe in hiring people who are better than me in certain areas. This includes considering their technical skills, experience, cultural fit, or adaptability. I am fortunate to have a highly diverse and exceptionally talented global leadership team. Over nearly five years, three out of our four business units, which we refer to as practices, have been led with great success by women. By assembling a team with diverse strengths and experiences, I can achieve a winning combination. Just as a symphony requires different instruments to make beautiful music, a great business team thrives on the unique abilities and contributions of its members.

The Occasional Bout of Micromanagement

Having assembled a talented team with diverse skills and experience, you will now be tempted to micromanage them. It's a constant leadership challenge because managing the team is what you're paid to do.

Let us imagine I am captaining a cruise ship. Each day, I consult the navigator and set our course and speed to get to where we're scheduled to be. I speak to the engineer and learn that all engines are humming along just as they should. I review the crew roster prepared by the first officer, and I'm satisfied that everyone knows where to be and what to do.

As the captain, I then show up on the bridge and ask if all is well. Of course, it is. The crew knows my expectations, and they perform them smoothly. So I go hobnob with the passengers, asking them how the cruise is going, whether the food is tasty, and if they're having fun aboard. I am, essentially, standing on the deck, watching the crew deliver, waiting for something out of the ordinary to happen. That can be a challenge, especially for a disruptive leader who is very hands-on. But my crew is a successful team, and the ship is going in the right direction, on course to the destination the passengers paid us to take them to.

I might then go hide in my cabin for a few hours to review the crew roster. We have an assistant engineer who wants to be a chief engineer, but she needs a training class before she can take the test. I make arrangements with the cruise line to get that training. Our ship's doctor is retiring in a few months, so I review resumes. Several passengers suggested improvements, so I wrote a report for the cruise line, agreeing with a few recommendations and disagreeing with others. I am doing what I alone can do while keeping one eye on what the crew can do.

Then the ship hits an unexpected storm. I head for the bridge and take command. I direct people: "Pilot set this course. Engineer, full power on all engines. Purser, get the passengers safely to their cabins." I tell them exactly what to do and send the first officer to make sure they do it. I will micromanage that situation until the ship navigates out of the storm and back into calm, safe seas.

As a leader, I find that maintaining focus on my specific responsibilities is the most effective way to avoid micromanaging others. My role is to empower, enable, train, and support team members in meeting the challenges of their several positions. This approach embodies servant leadership, where I prioritize serving their needs while ensuring progress in the right direction. However, when unexpected situations arise, I am not afraid to take bold and hands-on action and adapt accordingly. Most of the time, I serve my team members by allowing them the autonomy to excel in their roles. Their success reflects my own.

Making Tough Decisions

Leaders bear accountability for making well-informed, responsible decisions. They should consider both the short and long-term impacts, assess risks, consult with relevant stakeholders, and take ownership of the consequences of their choices. In the realm of disruptive leadership, when faced with difficult decisions, responsibility, ownership, and accountability are paramount. It's essential for leaders to embrace their responsibilities and take ownership of their actions in order to achieve success. When someone is trusted with responsibility, it gives them the authority to oversee and manage a venture and makes them accountable for the outcome.

I recognize that responsibility and accountability are essential for the success of my team. Each member must act responsibly to address all aspects of our work, leading to great achievements. The presence of an irresponsible individual or nonperforming team member can disrupt the equilibrium and burden others, resulting in a decline in morale. As a leader, I may face tough situations such as reassigning nonperforming team members, taking swift action for undesirable behaviors, motivating the team, optimizing organizational structures for efficiency, bringing in new talent, managing organizational politics, and protecting staff well-being.

As a leader committed to fostering teamwork, you may occasionally encounter situations where not everyone is on board. Some individuals may not participate or contribute at all. In such cases, if those individuals are genuinely in need of assistance, it's imperative to utilize all available resources to support them. However, if it becomes evident that they never had the intention to join your efforts and are actively working against your progress, it's crucial not to let them undermine the integrity of the entire team.

As a responsible leader dedicated to ensuring the success of your team, you may be compelled to take evasive action. This may involve making difficult decisions to let go of individuals who jeopardize the team's success. It's never easy to let go of people you care for. I don't like it at all, but it's necessary. By doing so, you safeguard the overall harmony and effectiveness of the team to allow growth and success to flourish.

Full Accountability to Stakeholders

Financial accountability to all stakeholders is crucial for disruptive leaders for several reasons.

First, disruptive ventures often requires significant financial investments and resources. Without proper accountability, leaders may find themselves facing financial risks and mismanagement, jeopardizing the success of their disruptive ventures. Second, founders play a significant role in attracting investors, partners, and stakeholders. These individuals or entities will scrutinize the financial health and accountability of the leader and their organization before committing their support. Demonstrating financial transparency and responsibility builds trust and confidence, making it easier to secure necessary funding and partnerships.

I recognize the importance of partnering with CFOs at both the enterprise and business levels. In fact, CFOs have been crucial in my last two disruptive ventures within large organizations, serving as major sponsors. They helped navigate the complexities of summarizing progress in financial terms and effectively communicated with the executive team and the board.

When situations did not go as planned, the CFOs I worked with closely, such as Tony Young of KPMG and Phil Bradley of GHD, proved to be invaluable. They not only provided financial solutions but also facilitated effective communication with stakeholders. Phil, an immensely seasoned CFO and outstanding strategic thinker, emerged as my sponsor as we embarked on the path to establishing GHD Digital. His visionary outlook and talent for inspiring innovative thoughts were truly exceptional. During the nascent stages of our groundbreaking venture, Phil consistently backed me, offering invaluable support and guidance. Thanks to Tony's and Phil's altruistic backing, our professional bond blossomed into a lifelong friendship that I deeply cherish. Overall, financial accountability is not only crucial for the success of disruptive leaders but also for building trust and establishing strong relationships with stakeholders. Collaborating with experienced CFOs can provide the necessary guidance and support to navigate the complexities of driving entrepreneurship in large, complex global organizations.

Ensuring Transparency and Honesty in Communication

Disruptive leader accountability for communication is another crucial tool in today's fast-paced and rapidly evolving business landscape. Such leaders recognize that effective communication is critical to building trust, fostering collaboration, and driving organizational success. They proactively take responsibility for ensuring that communication flows smoothly throughout the organization, leading by example and setting a high standard for others to follow. Focusing on open, transparent communication is essential, particularly when discussing challenging topics. Not only does it foster a sense of comfort among others, but it also cultivates trust. Conversely, any leaders who resort to selective information or disclosure in an attempt to manipulate others toward distrust will soon lose respect and trust within the organization.

One example of a disruptive leader who exemplifies accountability for communication is Microsoft CEO Satya Nadella. When Nadella took over as CEO in 2014, he recognized the need for a cultural transformation within the company. He implemented several initiatives to foster open communication and transparency, such as conducting company-wide Q&A sessions, where employees could ask him direct questions about the company's vision and direction. Nadella also started sharing more information about the company's strategy and goals to ensure that employees were aligned and had a clear understanding of their roles and responsibilities. This commitment to communication and transparency significantly contributed to Microsoft's resurgence as a tech industry leader.

Disruptive leaders who prioritize accountability for communication understand that only when they are open with others can others be open with them.

Managing Business Risks

Disruptive leadership is not reckless leadership.

Disruptive leaders must carefully manage risks to navigate the challenges they face. Whether it involves decisions on investing money, manpower, or other resources, they must carefully assess and mitigate risks. They also need to proactively address potential reputational risks that may arise from their disruptive actions. We do not want advancement at the cost of another's reputation or success.

Recognizing the importance of embracing risks and accepting the inevitability of mistakes is far more beneficial than succumbing to inaction entirely. Remaining stagnant within the confines of safety inhibits us from attaining significant progress. It's solely through the audacity to take risks and the humbling lessons we glean from our missteps that we can genuinely advance and reach new heights. Throughout my journey, I've learned the importance of avoiding defensiveness when facing my own mistakes. Instead, I embrace accountability, taking ownership, and rectifying any negative impact caused.

I passionately defend my team when unjustly treated, yet I understand the difference between defending with conviction and becoming defensive—that is, blocking critique. Managing risks is not a one-time event for disruptive leaders. It's an ongoing process. They must remain vigilant, anticipating and adapting to emerging risks as they continue to drive innovation and challenge conventional practices. This necessitates staying up to date with market trends, engaging with relevant stakeholders, and developing contingency plans to mitigate potential negative outcomes.

In addition, disruptive leaders must strike a balance between being courageous risk-takers and being responsible stewards of their organizations. This involves weighing the potential rewards against the risks and considering both short-term gains and long-term sustainability.

Successfully managing risks allows disruptive leaders to navigate the uncertain terrain with confidence, ensuring that their actions are aligned with their strategic objectives and minimizing potential detrimental consequences. By embracing a proactive and informed approach to risk management, these leaders can maintain their competitive edge and continue driving positive change in their industries.

Harry Truman, president of the United States from 1945 to 1953, had a small sign on his desk. It said simply, "The Buck Stops Here." It always has and always will. There's no blaming others for failure. Leaders delegate responsibilities to their team members, who are accountable to the team for their individual results, but the duty to upper echelons falls squarely on the person in the center chair. A leader must "walk the talk" so their team members can follow, for the team will emulate their leader's behavior. The disruptive leader is accountable for how they lead the team and for their successes and failures.

CHAPTER 9
Turning the Seven Keys

Fear is the mind-killer.
—Frank Herbert

I started this book by saying the world is changing, and the pace of change has increased. Well, it's always been changing, and every disruptive change we've seen in the last one hundred years has brought new opportunities as well as new challenges.

Today, leaders must choose optimism as their guiding force. Instead of succumbing to fear of the unknown future, they should wholeheartedly embrace it. Opting for a proactive stance over a reactive one, they must be determined to exert influence over the inevitable changes that lie ahead.

You've all heard the old saying, "There are three types of people: Those who make things happen. Those who watch things happen. Those who wonder what happened." Those who see the challenges as opportunities prosper—in more ways than money! Those who watch, wonder, or are terrified may find themselves plowed under the challenges. I conclude this book by summarizing the power of the seven keys that I have evolved into my personal philosophy.

The Seven Keys

In the realm of complex business environments where we operate, the following seven keys transcend tradition and challenge conventional wisdom. These keys, born from a rich blend of lived experiences and keen observations, offer a pathway towards innovation and reinvention of ourselves and the organizations we lead. While they may initially provoke skepticism due to their departure from established norms of stability and uniformity, these keys are indispensable in navigating the turbulent waters impacting current business landscapes.

Embracing these keys heralds a new era of leadership—one that dares to defy convention and conventional expectations. The current age-old management practices can coexist with proposed leadership keys, as both serve different purposes—one short term and the other long term. This book is not a discourse on current management practices; rather, it shines a spotlight on the essential characteristics of leadership required to survive and thrive in today's world.

True leadership, I firmly believe, emerges beyond the confines of the ordinary. In a world where complacency and incremental progress fall short, these keys serve as beacons of guidance for those willing to chart a course toward extraordinary achievement. For leaders yearning to wield genuine influence and inspire greatness within their teams and organizations, the embrace of these keys is not just recommended—it is imperative. Failing to embrace new ways of thinking because they seem unconventional could significantly jeopardize the success of the organizations under our leadership. Those who wholeheartedly embrace these keys will witness a paradigm shift in their worldview, unlocking solutions to existing and emerging challenges while crafting a resilient strategy to combat disruptive forces.

1) Develop a Disruptive Mindset

Developing a disruptive mindset is a transformative process involving challenging norms, embracing change, fostering innovation, and building strong relationships. It is a journey of self-discovery, growth, and continuous improvement that shapes not only the individual but also the organizations and communities they influence.

The foundation of developing a disruptive mindset lies in questioning the status quo, challenging conventional thinking, and daring to think differently. By breaking free from traditional limitations and embracing a mindset of innovation and creativity, individuals can unlock their full potential and drive meaningful change. This shift in thinking allows leaders to approach challenges with a fresh perspective, explore new possibilities, and create innovative solutions that have a lasting impact.

Embracing the uncertainty of an unpredictable and complex world is key to adapting to the rapidly changing dynamics of today's business environment. It requires a willingness to challenge ingrained beliefs, remain open to new perspectives, and continuously seek personal growth. By fostering self-awareness and actively challenging mental programming, individuals can overcome limitations and uncover new ways of thinking, problem-solving, and living a more fulfilling life.

Building a disruptive mindset also involves daring to dream big and take calculated risks. Visionary leaders push boundaries, challenge assumptions, and pursue audacious goals that inspire others to rally behind a common purpose. By communicating their big dreams, leaders attract top talent, foster resilience, and create a culture of innovation that propels organizations to new heights of success.

Furthermore, developing a disruptive mindset entails building high-impact relationships, driving bold transformational change, and differentiating oneself from the crowd. Effective leadership requires collaborating with diverse individuals, enlisting team members for change, communicating clearly, planning for quick wins, and prioritizing personal growth. By embracing risk-taking, fostering innovation, defining a unique value proposition, and telling a compelling story, leaders can establish credibility, inspire others, drive change, and leave a lasting impact on their organizations and communities.

In conclusion, the journey of developing a disruptive mindset is a continuous process of growth, self-discovery, and transformation. It involves challenging norms, embracing change, fostering innovation, and building strong relationships to drive meaningful progress and create a positive impact. By daring to think differently, dreaming big, taking risks, and communicating effectively, disruptive leaders can shape a better future and leave a lasting legacy that inspires others to follow in their footsteps.

2) Find a Disruptive Higher Purpose

In essence, leadership is the sense of calling to a higher purpose.

—Amit Ray

During crises like the COVID-19 pandemic, a clear higher purpose acts as a guiding light, offering direction, unity, and motivation to navigate challenges effectively. Companies that uphold their core values aligned with a higher purpose, support employees, and focus on societal impacts foster loyalty and engagement, empowering them to adapt and thrive amid uncertainty. By embracing a disruptive higher purpose, organizations can attract exceptional talent driven by a shared commitment to creating a positive impact.

To balance profits and a higher purpose, companies must integrate purpose-driven strategies that align financial success with social good. Disruptive leaders must establish and communicate the higher purpose effectively, fostering a culture that values both financial success and societal impact.

In attracting and retaining exceptional talent, a disruptive higher purpose plays a vital role in providing meaningful work, aligning values, creating a sense of impact, supporting personal growth, strengthening employee engagement, and differentiating from competitors. A higher purpose empowers employees, enhances the company's reputation, and fosters long-term sustainability, creating an environment that appeals to individuals seeking purpose-driven careers.

Further, a disruptive higher purpose inspires individuals and organizations to think big, make bold moves, and challenge existing norms to create significant positive change. By integrating purpose, values, and actions, companies can create a sustainable, impactful business model that delivers financial success while promoting social good. Ultimately, embracing a disruptive higher purpose enables individuals and organizations to matter, make a difference, and live well by contributing meaningfully to the world in impactful ways.

3) Get Out of Your Comfort Zone

> *Comfort is your biggest trap and coming out of your comfort zone is your biggest challenge.*
>
> *—Manoj Arora*

Your higher purpose will make people uncomfortable, but you are going to do it regardless.

Embarking on a transformative journey by challenging the familiar confines of comfort zones has the potential to reshape beliefs and steer the course of our lives. It is a journey that uncovers a profound truth often overlooked: individuals who dare to push their limits deserve admiration for embodying exceptional strength, resilience, and an unwavering pursuit of passions above self-interest. Disruptive leaders actively seek out challenges, rejecting mediocrity and embracing adversity with relentless determination. By stepping outside their comfort zones and prioritizing service to others, they epitomize the immense potential within us all.

Living comfortably in today's world represents a modern luxury vastly different from the historical norm of constant discomfort endured by our ancestors for over 2.5 million years. Finding solace in the present often generates a fear of the unknown, hindering individuals from venturing beyond safe spaces to pursue growth. True progress arises when familiar boundaries are surpassed, fostering personal and professional advancement. Venturing beyond these limits demands a willingness to confront uncertainty, embrace change, and cultivate resilience in the face of challenges. Through expanding these boundaries progressively, individuals unlock new avenues for growth and self-improvement.

In the face of today's rapidly evolving landscape, both leaders and organizations must break free from their comfort zones and welcome disruptive change. By nurturing a culture that thrives on continuous growth, learning, and innovation, leaders can effectively navigate challenges, unearth fresh possibilities, and position themselves for long-term success. Overcoming mental barriers, managing ego, making tough decisions, and honing new skills are fundamental strategies that drive individuals towards personal and professional advancement, enabling them to forge a future that transcends conventional boundaries.

Personal experiences have taught me that confronting fears head-on, proactively solving problems, and seizing growth opportunities are pivotal in stepping outside comfort zones. By challenging complacency, refining my leadership approach, and embracing constructive dissatisfaction, I have unleashed the full potential for transformative change within organizations. I firmly believe that vigorously pushing boundaries beyond comfort zones not only catalyzes unprecedented personal growth and resilience but also establishes a legacy that surpasses current limitations.

4) Build Relationships That Foster Disruptive Thinking

In any role, you build trusted relationships only if there is an alignment with your higher purpose.

In the context of cultivating disruptive relationships for success, businesses that prioritize a disruptive higher purpose showcase superior performance compared to those fixated solely on profits. By placing emphasis on employee well-being and nurturing strong relationships, a culture of loyalty is established where employees align their interests with those of the company. The cornerstone of robust relationships not only drives financial success and overall achievement but also underscores the critical importance of fostering a people-centric corporate environment.

Establishing trustworthy relationships extends beyond internal stakeholders to encompass a wide spectrum of crucial partners—from the board, investors, and partners to vendors and other key players. Effective leaders excel in cultivating strong networks within their teams and the broader ecosystem, reaping benefits that include inspiring individuals, mobilizing resources, overcoming obstacles, catalyzing collaborative innovation, and building credibility and trust.

Disruptive relationships serve as catalysts for personal growth by actively seeking feedback, sharing goals, learning from experiences, engaging in candid conversations, leveraging positive influences, collaborating and acquiring knowledge collectively, and seeking support during challenging moments. They facilitate constructive dialogues that propel success and foster innovative solutions.

Embracing vulnerability as a strength in leadership not only fosters personal growth but also nurtures trust within relationships. Confronting obstacles such as short-term thinking, cultural disparities, unhealthy competition, overreliance on technology, and viewing individuals as mere commodities is crucial in cultivating disruptive relationships.

Breaking down these barriers, shifting mindsets, and prioritizing collaboration, inclusivity, human connections, and the value of individuals are vital steps in building disruptive relationships. Building disruptive relationships and networks opens doors to new opportunities and resources, contributing significantly to both personal and professional advancement.

5) Disrupt the Status Quo

The highest calling of leadership is to challenge the status quo and unlock the potential of others. We need a leader who will lead the resurgence of this great nation and unlock its potential once again.

—Carly Fiorina

In today's fast-paced and ever-evolving world, the concept of disrupting the status quo has become a cornerstone of successful leadership. The entrenched state of affairs, also known as the status quo, often perpetuates complacency, hinders innovation, and stifles growth. This book delves into the significance of challenging traditional norms, embracing change, and fostering a culture of disruptive leadership. At the core of disrupting the status quo lies the intrinsic desire to challenge conventional thinking, question established practices, and envision new solutions to existing problems. The Latin terms *status quo*, *stare decisis*, and *torpor* encapsulate the essence of the current state of affairs, adherence to precedent, and complacency, respectively. While stability and tradition offer a sense of security, they can also lead to stagnation and inhibit progress.

In the contemporary business landscape, characterized by rapid digital transformation and relentless innovation, disrupting the status quo is imperative for survival and relevance. Traditional business models are being upended by agile startups and technology behemoths, emphasizing the importance of adaptability, creativity, and forward-thinking leadership. True disruptive leaders possess the courage to challenge norms, embrace unconventional thinking, and drive organizational change.

This book explores various reasons why managers and organizations tend to cling to the status quo, such as hierarchy, bureaucracy, nostalgia, herd mentality, and risk aversion. These factors can impede progress, limit innovation, and thwart growth potential. However, by adopting strategies to challenge the status quo, visionary, disruptive leaders can drive meaningful change and unlock new opportunities.

Creating a bold vision, enlisting key stakeholders' support, fostering critical thinking, providing data-driven insights, identifying white spaces for innovation, leveraging technology, and mustering courage are highlighted as essential strategies for disrupting the status quo. By engaging diverse perspectives, empowering teams, and embracing calculated risks, leaders can navigate uncharted territories, break free from conventional constraints, and carve out new paths for success. Resilience, perseverance, and bravery will help leaders confront opposition and overcome challenges while remaining committed to a disruptive vision. By embracing change, fostering a culture of experimentation, and valuing feedback, leaders can inspire their teams to challenge the status quo, drive innovation, and unlock untapped value.

Ultimately, the quest to disrupt the status quo is a journey of self-discovery, innovation, and transformation. By daring to dream the impossible, challenging the unbeatable, and striving for excellence, disruptive leaders can leave a lasting impact, reshape industries, and create a better future for themselves and their organizations. In a world that constantly demands evolution and adaptation, disruptive leadership emerges as a beacon of progress, resilience, and visionary thinking.

In conclusion, disrupting the status quo is not merely a choice but a necessity for leaders seeking to thrive in today's dynamic landscape. By embracing change, challenging norms, and fostering a culture of innovation, disruptive leaders can propel their organizations toward success and significance. As the world evolves and demands transformation, the disruptive leader stands poised to lead the charge, inspire change, and unlock unparalleled value in unexpected places.

6) Mental Resilience: Conquering Complacency and Fragility

Many times, the thought of fear itself is greater than what it's we fear.

—Idowu Koyenikan

In today's post-COVID landscape, marked by volatility and unpredictability, disruptive leaders are tasked with navigating uncharted territories. As the global dynamics shift due to unprecedented challenges, addressing mental fragility and complacency emerges as a critical necessity.

Disruptive leaders, known for their visionary outlook and innovative strategies, must recognize that their success hinges not only on external factors but also on their internal strength and resilience. The turbulent nature of the current environment necessitates that leaders understand their own mental state and prioritize the well-being of their teams. The psychological toll of prolonged uncertainty and rapid change is evident, with mental fragility–a vulnerability to stress, anxiety, and burnout–taking its toll on leaders within this new reality.

Mental fragility in leaders signifies a susceptibility that arises when confronted with multiple personal and professional challenges. Failure to address this vulnerability can impair decision-making, stifle innovation, and cloud a leader's vision. It is imperative for disruptive leaders to confront their vulnerabilities, encourage self-reflection, and safeguard their emotional equilibrium to face adversity with clarity and resolve.

Complacency presents an equally perilous threat in this dynamic environment. Leaders who fail to adapt risk falling into inertia if they cannot keep pace with the swiftly changing world. Complacency may stem from a fear of the unknown or the weight of multifaceted challenges. To combat this, leaders must actively cultivate a growth mindset, embrace continuous learning, and foster personal development. By nurturing mental flexibility and adaptability, leaders can sidestep complacency and flourish amidst uncertainty.

Addressing mental fragility and complacency extends beyond the individual–it impacts the entire organization. A team's strength is intricately linked to the resilience of its leader.

The challenges of mental complacency and fragility in a post-COVID world require proactive strategies for leaders to adapt and thrive. By fostering a culture of continuous learning, promoting self-awareness, encouraging feedback, igniting meaningful conversations, embracing diversity and inclusion, and actively challenging mental barriers, disruptive leaders can rise above complacency and fragility. These strategies empower leaders to navigate uncertainties, drive innovation, and foster a resilient organizational culture in the face of unprecedented challenges.

By prioritizing mental well-being, fostering personal growth, embracing change, nurturing self-awareness, and building a robust support system, leaders can conquer mental fragility and complacency. With a proactive approach to mental resilience, leaders can pave the way for success and growth in today's fast-paced and uncertain environment.

7) Disrupt What Accountability Means and Why Results Matter

Accountability means to say what you do, do what you say.

—Pearl Zhu

Disruptive leaders' accountability extends beyond their immediate team to their company, industry, community, and global stakeholders. This accountability entails personal responsibility for actions, decisions, and behavior, encompassing moral and ethical obligations.

There are two key aspects to a disruptive leader's accountability: personal and business. Personal accountability involves taking ownership of actions, decisions, and consequences without making excuses, while business accountability includes evaluating business operations for success and alignment with the established vision and goals. By embracing both personal and business accountability, disruptive leaders establish a foundation of trust, transparency, and ethical behavior essential for organizational success.

Accountabilities unique to disruptive leaders include justifying larger investments in innovation, managing business risks, fostering diversity, and ensuring transparent communication. These leaders emphasize vision and strategy, talent management, customer focus, innovation, financial management, risk management, stakeholder management, learning and adaptability, and ethical conduct. While similar to other business leaders, disruptive leaders operate within a distinct context that requires them to navigate uncertainties and drive change effectively.

Through accountability, disruptive leaders create a culture of excellence, recognize achievements, and drive innovation and growth within their organizations. They must make tough decisions, manage business risks proactively, and ensure full accountability to stakeholders. By empowering the right teams, embracing diversity, and communicating transparently, disruptive leaders set a high standard for organizational success. Recognizing the importance of managing risks and maintaining open communication, disruptive leaders lead with courage, integrity, and a commitment to driving positive change in their industries.

Ultimately, accountability is at the core of a disruptive leader's success, guiding them in navigating challenges, fostering innovation, and driving sustainable outcomes.

Communities Built by Disruptive Leaders Shape Futures

Communities built by disruptive leaders play a crucial role in shaping our future. These leaders understand that community-building is a gradual process, requiring consistent effort every day. Effective communication is key to building communities, encouraging a two-way exchange of knowledge and experiences between individuals, and fostering mutual growth and learning opportunities. By sharing both professional expertise and personal stories, community members forge deeper connections and create a reservoir of shared memories that solidify their bonds.

In a business environment, while disruptive leaders aspire to catalyze shifts in mindset and behavior, they also remain grounded in addressing practical business considerations. High-performance teams are crucial for community-building. Monitoring team performance, financial metrics, and adherence to priorities are essential aspects that ensure operational success. This is how disruptive leaders translate innovative ideas into tangible products or services that drive profitability and sustainability. Furthermore, community building needs them to prioritize holistic well-being, recognizing the significance of physical, mental, spiritual, and emotional health in maintaining peak professional performance for themselves and their team.

Building inclusive and efficient communities requires active engagement across various internal and external spheres, aiming to replace outdated practices with innovative solutions that cater to modern needs. These communities strive to cultivate a more understanding and inclusive society through collective efforts where diverse pathways to success are embraced and celebrated.

Calls to Action Are Many Times Double

The illiterate of the twenty-first century will not be those who cannot read or write; they will be those who cannot learn, unlearn, and relearn.

–Alvin Toffler

This book was written for individuals currently leading or aspiring to lead, striving to liberate themselves from conventional norms and adopt a courageous approach to leadership.

It does not intend to alienate those who are not yet prepared to assume leadership roles, steering clear of any notions of division or judgment, avoiding any notion of an "us or them" or "good versus bad" framework. It's important to discern between adept followers and adept leaders. Skilled followers may find solace in the comfort of the status quo, yet they remain open to supporting a leader who envisions a broader horizon of possibilities.

The conventional paradigms of leadership are losing relevance at an astonishing pace, making room for fresh and evolving approaches. If your ultimate ambition is to become a leader, adopting the disruptive mindset can reshape your trajectory toward success.

To navigate the ever-changing landscape of modern business and society, a disruptive leader must grasp the needs of all stakeholders. Employees, contractors, suppliers, distributors, retailers, consumers, industry regulators, and supportive associations are affected by what you do. Understanding their requirements is paramount to achieving the greatest success for the greatest number. Comprehending the unique needs of individual persons or groups means you can guide, support, inspire them, and empower them to envision and achieve your shared goals.

In the twenty-first century, leadership goes beyond ownership, management, political appointments, or elected roles. While some may view terms like "thought leader" and "influencer" as divisive, they are now integral and enduring attributes of effective leadership. Many thought leaders and influencers have achieved remarkable prominence in recent times.

In the past, intimate face-to-face exchanges within limited spaces were instrumental in building relationships. Yet the landscape has shifted dramatically in today's era, where connectivity thrives predominantly in the online realm, spanning across diverse platforms. As leaders navigating this digital age, understanding the multifaceted interests of our audience is paramount when disseminating information on social media. It's crucial to recognize that our virtual followers stem from all corners of the globe, converging here due to a shared belief in the value of our insights. The realm of leadership has expanded beyond traditional business spheres to encompass community domains, with social media emerging as an unparalleled stage for leaders to connect and interact with their followers in unprecedented ways.

Here are four things to keep in mind as you navigate this new space:

- Let go of the outdated leadership models you were once taught and held dear. Equip yourself with new skills and adapt to the evolving expectations of those you lead.
- Embrace the seven keys to disruptive leadership. Let them play a pivotal role in your approach in the twenty-first century.
- Find ways to use them based on your perspective and experience. Don't be bound by my experience. Allow my insights to inform and advise you but not to define you. Cultivate your own personal, disruptive mindset.
- Continuously evaluate and seek feedback on your effectiveness as a disruptive leader. Embrace opportunities for assessment and adjustment.

As you embark on your leadership journey, remember that there may be other important mindset shifts waiting for you. Continuously growing as a leader will reveal these to you, too. When you do discover them, do not hesitate to share your insights with me and others. Together, by becoming better leaders ourselves and empowering others to lead, we can create a significant and meaningful impact on the world.

Remember, this journey begins with you before it extends to those who follow you or your organization. It's crucial to have a clear understanding of your personal path before guiding others on theirs. The individual journey precedes the collective one.

Lead to disrupt!

Best of luck in all your future endeavors!

About the Author

Kumar R. Parakala, a global business leader and entrepreneur, embarked on his entrepreneurial journey at the young age of twenty-three when he established a training and consulting firm in Australia to fund his studies. Since then, he has successfully helped launch and scale technology and consulting enterprises worldwide from inception to multibillion-dollar success.

Over the last three decades, Kumar has served as a trusted advisor to CEOs, board directors, executives, prime ministers and premiers, academics, and military leaders on topics such as business growth, national security, digital transformation, artificial intelligence, technology risks, and governance. He has served on the faculties of leading universities and received several awards for his accomplishments.

Passionate about guiding our society and leaders through disruptive technological shifts, Kumar is a USA Today best-selling author. His thought leadership resonates with leaders in more than seventy countries and has been featured in top media outlets, including *Bloomberg, Wall Street Journal, Forbes, The Economist, Financial Times,* CNN, and CNBC.

By purchasing this book, you are supporting future leaders and budding artists. Proceeds benefit GHD Foundation and Musical Bridges Around the World (MWAB), fostering talent and positive societal impact.

www.ingramcontent.com/pod-product-compliance
Lightning Source LLC
Chambersburg PA
CBHW022221090526
44585CB00013BB/676